THE SUCCESSFUL TEACHING SERIES

CHILDREN: **THE LIVELY LEARNERS**

LAWRENCE O. RICHARDS, PH.D.

David C. Cook Publishing Co.
ELGIN, ILLINOIS/WESTON, ONTARIO

Acknowledgments

Appreciation is due Elsiebeth McDaniel, specialist in Christian education of young children, author, and consultant, for her contribution to this work.

Note: The first edition of this book appeared under the title, *You and Children*.

Published by David C. Cook Publishing Co.
850 N. Grove Ave., Elgin, IL 60120
Cable address: DCCOOK

Designer: Dawn Lauck
Cover illustration: Rowan Barnes-Murphy
Printed in U.S.A.
Library of Congress Catalog Card Number: 87-063567
ISBN: 1-55513-184-0

CONTENTS

CHAPTER ONE
WHY TEACH CHILDREN?

▶Sunday School is a school of the heart as well as of the mind. Adults aren't the only ones who have needs that must be met by the Lord. So do children. Trusting and personally experiencing God do not suddenly come into style when a person reaches the teen years.

Don has an effective witness on the college campus. He loves the Lord, studies His Word, teaches a Sunday School class, and is eager to witness. But Don is looking for something.

Don is searching to reconstruct his first knowledge of Jesus Christ, God, and the Bible.

Don says, "I know I made God a promise when I was in first grade, but I can't remember just what it was."

Don is trying to put the pieces together. He knows that when he was a child, Sunday School teachers explained the Word of God, invited him to receive Christ, and prayed for him. What Don wants now is information about his starting point. *How did I feel about God as a child?* he wonders.

Sam was 95 when he died. He had seen a lot of life, but he had really only lived 48 hours.

Two days before his death, Sam was visited in the hospital by his wife's pastor. There Sam received Christ as his Savior. The next day the pastor returned. He was amazed to hear Sam repeating Bible verses and trying to sing a hymn. As the pastor talked with the old man, he realized that Sam was not a complete novice about spiritual things. He did have some understanding of God's power and Heaven's reality.

The pastor said, "Sam, you only received Christ as your Savior yesterday, but you're quoting Scripture and talking about events that most converts can't understand. How is this?"

"Well, preacher, I went to Sunday School as a boy," said Sam. "Didn't like it too well, but I sure remember a lot. Now that I know the Lord Jesus is for real, it's all coming back."

Jeff is a theology student. While attending seminary, he works with inner-city youth. He knows kids who have been on drugs, some who have dropped out of school, and others who live according to the rules of gang warfare. Jeff is having many new experiences in sharing Christ.

Is part of Jeff's success due to the fact that from childhood he has walked with the Lord, day by day, year by year? Jeff is a product of a Christian home and a Christian education program sponsored by a church with dedicated teachers. Jeff draws on his home training, seminary education, and church experiences—Sunday School, weekday club, youth groups, Vacation Bible School, and camp. Jeff knows that he received Christ as a small child.

Sarah is a problem! She is the most talkative child in her fourth-grade Sunday School class. She can't sit still and seems to be constantly searching through her purse or those of her friends.

But walk with Sarah through the week. At public school she is known as a child who is honest, unselfish, and dependable. She is concerned about others and often volunteers to do helpful things at some sacrifice to herself. Why does she sacrifice to help others? Sarah would tell you, "Well, if you love the Lord like I do, you're supposed to do stuff like that."

Twelve-year-old Lori lives in a broken home. Her father loaded the kids in the car one day and drove off, leaving his wife. Lori doesn't know where her mother is. She knows her father is working two jobs so that his family can get along.

Lori is on her own much of the time. Her three older brothers do not pay much attention to her. Lori has many temptations, but she is trying to live as a child of God. One big help in Lori's life is her Sunday School teacher. Lori believes everything her teacher says and wants to be like her.

These are only five true case histories. What do they show? Obedience to the words of Jesus, who instructed His followers to be "teaching them to obey everything I have commanded you" (Mt. 28:20). They also illustrate God's faithfulness to His Word; those who prayerfully teach His Word can expect Him to bring the results.

Christian growth does not come in one big step. The Christian life begins with faith in Christ and develops through fellowship with Him, study and acceptance of His Word, and daily dependence on the Lord. God uses the past work of consecrated teachers even when an individual accepts Christ as an adolescent or an adult.

Children need to experience the Lord as only children can. There are spiritual things that only a child can fully appreciate. Who but a child really wonders how God made dandelion seeds that travel, clouds that hold water, and birds who know their way? Surely a child uniquely experiences the nearness of Christ when everyone else is bigger, older, and seems smarter. When we do not teach children, we deny them a child's experiences of the Lord—experiences an adult can never have.

Whether we think we are living in the greatest and most exciting days or the worst of days, a great need is to teach children. Children need to meet God. They need to see the Bible as reality. They need to respond to the Lord and discover joy in living as His child.

Although children are experiencing daily change in many forms, the basic purpose of churches seeking to minister to them remains the same. The local church must still fulfill the pattern given in Acts 2:41-47. The church should accomplish the following functions: (1) to educate, (2) to provide fellowship, (3) to worship, (4) to serve or minister, and (5) to evangelize. To merely bring a child to receive Christ as Savior is not enough. The all-inclusive aim of Christian education is "so that the man of God may be throughly equipped for every good work" (II Tim. 3:17).

Teaching for boys and girls should aim at leading children to respond to Christ as Savior. This purpose is basic. Lifelong commitment to Christ is only made following a child's realization of his or her personal sin. Then having become a member of God's family through faith in the redemptive work of Christ, the child is ready to grow in his or her new life.

But in answering the question, "Why teach children?" we must remember that not all children have reached the point of accountability. Some children, like Don, will not be ready to receive Christ before adolescence. These children deserve good spiritual "prenatal" care.

A child needs to be loved in order that he or she may learn to love. A child needs to experience faith and confidence in other persons so that he or she may come to have faith and confidence in the God those persons worship. More than one Christian educator has said that the adults who work with children represent 75 percent of the meaning of the word *church* to those children. Clarence H. Benson, cofounder of the Evangelical Teacher Training Association and prominent Christian educator, is credited with saying, "First I learned to love my teacher. Then I learned to love my teacher's Bible. And then I learned to love my teacher's Lord."

There is a particular challenge and blessing reserved for those who teach children. It is easy for some to want to teach high school or junior high young people, because this is the age when a teacher can see decisions made and acted on. A teacher does not see a young child, still under the guidance of his or her parents, taking big steps. A teacher may see a child taking small steps—daily prayer, gaining victory over fear, or determining to stop saying bad words. A high school teen is usually struggling to do what he or she wants; a child is struggling to do what he or she is told. How wonderful that our great Lord can meet the needs of both!

Why teach children? Because children are waiting for teachers! Almost every church has opportunities for teachers who will work with children—teachers who will become like children, identifying with children in their interests, needs, and problems. Children are waiting for teachers who can interpret the truths that Jesus taught, so that they can understand. Part of the purpose of this book is to help you be a teacher of children.

As we speak of teaching children, however, remember that a child is not *educated into* a positive response to God. Sufficient exposure to Bible teaching, directed by the Holy Spirit, helps a child want to respond to God. Then, when he or she is made ready by the Spirit of God, that child will receive Christ.

Why teach children? Because a child comes to Sunday School (or another church activity) for only one hour, but that hour becomes a part of the child. Our purpose in that hour is to help children live Bible truths, because the great objective in Christian education is the new person in Jesus Christ.

Because even a child is known by what he or she does, we are deeply concerned that children grow day by day in their ability to live the Christian life. Even children in early elementary grades should be increasingly able to solve their problems according to what God says. God has planned for adults—parents and teachers—to help children find the answers in the Bible and live by them.

But Christian growth on the part of a child does not just happen. God works through His Holy Spirit in the life of the child. God also works through the dedicated teacher who will plan and work toward the objectives that meet the spiritual needs of boys and girls.

REACT

1. What Sunday School teacher or church leader did you admire as a child? Why?
2. What do you wish you had learned as a child?

ACT

If you are a teacher, make a list of your pupils. Think of each child's personal potential and write it next to his or her name. Now pray daily for these children.

CHAPTER TWO
THE TEACHER

▶"You show that you are a letter from Christ, the result of our ministry, written not with ink but with the Spirit of the living God, not on tablets of stone but on tablets of human hearts" (II Cor. 3:3).

The apostle Paul emphasized that believers are to reveal Christ. Teachers in particular are "read" by many. They are more than communicators; they are also examples. They are keys to much of the success in the Sunday School. Programs, methods, and materials will all fail unless the teacher is "full of faith and of the Holy Spirit" (Acts 6:5), as were the early believers.

Why Teach?
Before exploring what a teacher is or should be, every teacher needs to examine his or her motives for teaching. What motivates a person to teach will clearly have an effect on him or her, and on the kind of teaching he or she does. There are many motives for teaching. Which of the following are yours?

- ▶I teach to support the work of the church.
- ▶I teach because I enjoy children.
- ▶I teach because I feel it is my duty.
- ▶I teach because someone taught me and I want to repay this debt.

- ▶I teach because all parents aren't Christians, and kids need to know and be influenced by adult Christians.
- ▶I teach because as a church member I should.
- ▶I teach because teachers are respected in my church. (Who is honest enough to check this reason?)
- ▶I teach because I feel that I'm doing something for the Lord.
- ▶I teach because a friend (pastor, etc.) asked me.
- ▶I teach because children ought to know the Bible.
- ▶I teach because someone taught my kids and now I want to do my part.
- ▶I teach because no one else seems to want to.

Are any of those reasons wrong? Probably not, but two big reasons have not been listed. Did you miss them? First, a teacher should want to learn and grow. This is a good motive for teaching boys and girls. The other motive omitted from the list relates to much more than teaching—a motive basic in our life with Christ. The motive is love—love for Christ, and love for others.

Love does not always burn with the same intensity—sometimes physical health, emotions, and circumstances affect the way we feel about the Lord. But every Christian recognizes the truth of I John 4:11, 12: "Dear friends, since God so loved us, we also ought to love one another . . . but if we love one another, God lives in us and his love is made complete in us." We find many more verses in the New Testament about love for God and for one another. When we teach because we love Jesus Christ, then we care about the persons we teach—care about them as individuals. Many people have been changed because they are aware that someone else cares about and believes in them.

The Holy Spirit can work through you to bring about changes in an individual's life, but your love for and belief in the individual may well prepare him or her for the work of the Holy Spirit.

There must be this kind of helpful relationship between a teacher and a pupil if learning is to take place that results in changes in the life of the pupil. "The child who identifies with his teacher through affection, admiration and submissiveness will 'take unto himself' not only what the teacher believes and teaches but also what he is and does" (Allan H. Jahsmann, *How You Too Can Teach*).

What Sunday School teachers do you remember? Which of their lessons do you recall? The chances are you do not remember very many specific lessons, but you do remember the adults for what they were. Probably those you remember with warm feelings respected you as a person, loved you, and tried to understand you. In Sunday School teaching, what the teacher is counts for a great deal. You may *speak* a Bible lesson, but your life also *teaches* what you say.

The teacher's life is especially important as children move into the years of middle childhood—eight to eleven. During the early years, every child believes his or her parents are absolutely right, that they know all the answers and can solve any problem. Then in middle childhood the child discovers that there are problems adults cannot solve. There is wrong that goes uncorrected. At this time the child is anxiously watching for the reaction of adults, discovering how they react to the world as he or she is coming to know it. How important that children be able to see teachers reacting according to their Christian beliefs—not compromising, but responding as examples of all believers.

The teacher's example either contradicts or emphasizes, adding exclamation points, to what he or she teaches. Every contact a teacher has leaves a mark on the child's life. The teacher and the teaching become part of the child.

This important chapter about the teacher precedes a chapter about children. This order was chosen because teachers need to decide what a teacher should be and do before they teach children. If a teacher does not have the best of motives, and is not willing to work at being a teacher, there is little point in finding out what boys and girls are like.

What Kind of Teacher?

Let's classify teachers as authoritarian, permissive, and democratic.

If we assume that the teacher is to be the authority, there are many problems. In the first place, God is the only authority. Then, too, the Christian life can be lived only on the basis of faith and close relationship with God. How can any individual teacher dare to be an authority on what he or she has not personally discovered? God plans tomorrow's experiences for each of His children. What He plans for you may not be at all the same as what He plans for your pupils. Your pupils must live in close, personal relationship with God; you cannot do this for them. Nor is the teacher to be an authority intruding between God and man. Jesus Christ, not the teacher, is the Mediator between God and man (I Tim. 2:5).

Teachers who think of themselves as authorities are more easily threatened; they feel insecure. They tend to dominate the class and think they must know all the answers. Their role is that of policemen, of disciplinarians in the poorest sense of the word. This type of teacher feels threatened when children are noisy, ask questions that cannot be answered, try to get attention in unapproved ways, and disagree with him or her.

The second type, the permissive teacher, is quite the opposite. Teachers of this type are very happy to have children in Sunday School; they may believe that their main function is to make children *like* Sunday School and the teachers. Therefore, they will let the children have fun and hesitate to enforce order in the classroom. They do not consider the time wasted as long as every child has a chance to talk.

Permissive teachers are not too concerned with specific goals. They seem to believe that everything will come out all right somehow. They have been given the responsibility to teach, but sidestep it. While they may think the class is enjoying the sessions, they would be surprised to discover that children want a sense of direction and need to feel they have accomplished something. Check the list under "Qualities of a good teacher" later in this chapter to see what children believe are important teacher characteristics. How does the permissive teacher measure up?

The third type of teacher fulfills a helpful role. Teachers from this mold are sensitive to the emotional needs of pupils in their groups. They want pupils to open up. They are guides who set the stage for learning and have ideas about how to accomplish it. They see their pupils as people, as partners in discovering God's answers. Pupils do not run over these teachers or usurp their authority, because these teachers have a respectful attitude toward every child. They listen to what pupils say. They do not have to adhere slavishly to a lesson plan, but can take time to answer students' questions. They are adaptable, depending on the Holy Spirit to help them see what their pupils need. They are guides, because they are prepared and able to create an atmosphere of discovery. They have had experience in the Christian life, but are also able to admit that there is much they do not know.

The democratic teacher is honest. Children respect honesty and sincerity. Have you ever heard adolescents remark about the hypocrisy of adults? Where did they get that idea? Is it possible that they began to think that way when they were children and found their teachers lacking in honesty, settling for pious answers that sounded right?

Most adults are not honest about themselves—their fears, limitations, weaknesses, prejudices, and motives. Some teachers present themselves to children as perfect—all-knowing, all-powerful, always rational, always just, and always right. This is the worst lie any teacher can tell about himself or herself. That may be strong language, but there is truth in it. Because we want children to conform to God's standards, we often impress them with unreality. By doing so, we make the Bible and God unreal.

Have you had fellow Christians give you quick answers when you wanted them to really *feel* with you? Suppose you were afraid of your first plane ride or trip to the hospital. Did you feel comforted when someone responded quickly, "I'll pray for you," or, "Trust the Lord, and don't fear"? You knew what was said was true, but you did want the person saying it to feel with you. You wanted some emotional reaction.

We need enough faith in God to be honest with our boys and girls. We want them to see us as real persons who are still learning to trust God.

What About Discipline?

Some of the most frequently asked questions in Sunday School workshops focus on discipline. "How can I keep the kids quiet?" "How can I teach reverence?" "How can I get the kids to show some respect?" All of these questions show that teachers feel threatened. Everything is not right in the classroom.

What is your attitude about discipline? Are you interested in it because it helps you have a quiet class, cover the lesson, or know what to do about some impossible child? Teachers are concerned about these things, but this should not be the sole reason for discipline.

Why is discipline being discussed in a chapter about the teacher? Isn't it the kids that cause the problems? Yes, they surely do. If a teacher had no pupils to teach, there would be no need to discipline. But as long as there are students, teachers must think about their own attitudes toward discipline in their classes. Discipline should not be considered a problem but a purpose in teaching. Discipline—self-control—becomes a part of the learning process.

A teacher needs to grow in his or her own self-control and obedience to God. Then he or she is in a position to help children develop self-control. If we think of discipline as self-control, we will not think of it as "Doing as you're told without asking any questions."

How much self-control do the children in your class need to exert? Enough so that every pupil can participate and can learn. What kind of atmosphere have you set up? What kind of teaching are you doing? This has something to do with the kind of discipline each child aspires to. If yours is a teacher-controlled class, where the pupils must listen to all you say and wait for permission to speak, they should exercise the amount of self-control needed in this situation. If yours is a permissive class, where everyone gets into the act and you hope and pray that some learning is taking place, the children need not exercise much self-control. Children soon learn how adults expect them to behave. They decide to behave on the basis of what they have to gain or lose.

There are some definite things that a teacher can do to maintain a good learning atmosphere, helping the children develop self-control. Some of these suggestions come from public school teachers, others from experienced Sunday School teachers.

1. Don't expect too much from the children. Recognize individual needs and age-group characteristics. Sometimes children exhibit lack of control because methods or materials are above or below their abilities and interest.
2. Keep the classroom itself interesting and conducive to order.
3. Plan activities so that students are occupied from the minute they come into the Sunday School room.
4. Don't talk so much that children become restless.
5. In a group of ten or less, try to give every student some attention every week, speaking directly to each student.
6. Friends are bound to talk to each other. If this disturbs the class, assign seats.
7. Let pupils know why they must not be noisy. Don't settle for statements such as, "This is God's house."
8. Come to class prepared to teach. This means a prayerfully prepared lesson. The teacher who lets the class fool around at the beginning cannot expect that class to suddenly come to order and turn to the Bible lesson.

9. Set a standard for behavior in your class.
10. Try some of the following statements and questions to help students develop self-control without embarrassing the individual:
    a. When you are all sitting quietly, we'll have our story.
    b. John, will you and James try to keep two chairs between you? You may put things on the chairs, but let's not have anyone sit there.
    c. Matt, if you sit in the front row, you'll be able to see the visuals better.
    d. Chris, did you have something you wanted to say? (This must be said sincerely.)
    e. Joan, are you comfortable, or would you like to take this chair?
    f. Tim, do you have a Bible to read from?
11. Be firm. Remember, firmness must be motivated from concern that all in the group be able to learn.
12. Don't try to outtalk a student. Raising your voice, except in rare instances, will have little effect. If you stop talking or lower your voice, the pupil is likely to pay attention.

Qualities of a Good Teacher

Good teachers are not born, but are made through conscientious effort. Jesus took His disciples with Him and trained them. He will train anyone whom He has called to teach. In Christ's training program, the teacher learns to teach God's Word as the Holy Spirit applies and personalizes the Word in the pupils' lives. The teacher cannot do the work of the Holy Spirit, but can develop a knowledge of the Word of God, a relationship to Christ, methods of teaching, and an understanding of the pupils.

The qualities that make good teachers begin with the

teachers themselves; it is not so much what they do or say, but what they are.

The following points are considered very important by many children. These qualities of a good teacher are not necessarily in order of importance.

1. Happy, cheerful, "smiley," likes fun
2. Treats you well—does not think you are a baby
3. Sees something good in everyone
4. Doesn't get mad when you don't know something
5. Is fair to everyone—doesn't have "pets" or like boys better than girls
6. Knows what he or she is talking about
7. Wants to help you
8. Willing to let you explain what you know and think

There are also other important factors for the Sunday School teacher:

1. The teacher must believe in the Book he or she teaches and be growing in Bible knowledge and Christian experience.
2. The teacher must believe in boys and girls. Any teacher who does not like children should consider resigning. Children read their teachers. One child said, "She says she likes us, but when she pushes the kids around, I know she doesn't."
3. The teacher must believe in prayer, because he or she must pray for himself or herself and for every child in the class.
4. A teacher should be willing to work and learn.

Jesus loved each person and showed concern for each individual's interests and needs. As human beings, we may find it impossible to like every child equally, but a dedicated teacher can truthfully say, "I do my best for every child." Whether you personally like a child or not, that child has a potential for growth and response to God. Your part is to teach so that the child has an opportunity to respond to the Lord.

Teachers need to have a clear vision of the results they want to achieve. Of course every born-again teacher wants to see pupils come to Christ and grow in faith, but this is the overall aim of all Christian education in your church. What are the specific results you want for your class? You should be able to determine results through knowledge of your pupils' needs and the aims or emphases given in the curriculum you are using.

A teacher can feel secure when he or she can affirm, *God has led me into teaching; God will work through me; even though I fail at times, God is still in control of my teaching and He will bring results; I am more interested in helping my children live Bible truth than I am in what they think of me; I am teaching God's Word which is infallible; and I know how Bible truth relates to everyday living.*

The Test of a Successful Teacher

It is difficult to test Sunday School teaching because learning, as defined in this book, is living Bible truth. Knowing Bible facts is not the measure of success.

Think of any test you've taken that required factual recall. How did you get a passing grade? Was it not a case of drill, drill, drill, or review, review, review? Perhaps you made up flash cards with formulas or facts on them. When you finally passed, what did you do? Very often when a person passes a subject that demands recall of factual knowledge, he or she celebrates by destroying the material that helped! The high school student tosses a marked-up textbook into the river; the college student tears review sheets to shreds, saying,

"Well, that's out of the way." This isn't the way we want to judge Christian education.

If you have taught a long time, or will teach for some years, you have seen (or will see) results in the lives of your pupils. Often the Lord in His goodness lets us know the results of our work. But a Christian teacher cannot always measure his or her effectiveness. One teacher sows, another reaps, but God receives the glory. This is as it should be! Even though you do not see the results of your teaching, you will have the blessing that comes from obedience to God. This is the way we must evaluate our teaching.

REACT

1. Do you think it is important that every child should like you? Is it important that you like every child—or that you want to do your best for each child?
2. Are your motives for teaching included in the list given at the beginning of the chapter? Are you satisfied with your motives?

ACT

1. You may have taught one particular age-group for many years—first graders, for example—and will for many more. However, this is the only year you will have the children who are in your class *now.* Recall their names. Are you satisfied with the "marks" you are making on these children?
2. Read I John 4. How well does it describe your present attitude toward God and your students?

CHAPTER THREE
THE CHILDREN: IN THE PROCESS OF BECOMING

▶The Lord Jesus is keenly interested in our understanding children. He said, "Whoever welcomes one of these little children in my name welcomes me"(Mk. 9:37). Children hold the future of the world in their hands, and our commitment to the Lord directs us to help them come to know Him.

Children are not miniature adults. They are human beings who will some day become adults after they too have passed through the various stages of physical and mental growth. With the help of Christian parents and teachers and the ministry of the Holy Spirit, they will grow spiritually. What a challenge to help them! What a tragedy to put any obstruction in the way of their coming to know Christ and live for Him. "And whoever welcomes a little child like this in my name welcomes me. But if anyone causes one of these little ones who believe in me to sin, it would be better for him to have a large millstone hung around his neck and to be drowned in the depths of the sea" (Mt. 18:5, 6).

After a child is born into the physical world, he or

she needs to be born into the Kingdom of God through the new birth. Jesus said to a wise teacher who came to see Him, "You must be born again" (Jn. 3:7). Christian parents and teachers can influence a child to respond to God. How? Through the example of their Christian lives, through prayer, and through loving and understanding the child.

As you begin this chapter, you already know the kind of teacher you want to be. This chapter will help you discover and appreciate the children you teach.

To understand children you can: (1) memorize lists of characteristics for each age—six through eleven; (2) watch children; and (3) teach children. But too many teachers forget that one of the best ways to understand children is to listen, listen, listen to them! In this chapter you will find generalizations about children, some age characteristics that apply to elementary school children, and principles that help teachers listen.

In many ways children are the same today as they were 50 years ago, but in many other ways, children are different. What did you like to do as a child? Do children engage in that same activity today? Think in what ways the same activity, if children do it, is different. For example, they read, but the books are not the ones you read as a child. Was popcorn a treat to you? What was? What is a treat to the children you teach? What did you do for entertainment when you were a child? Are children doing the same thing today? These are just a few of the obvious ways in which children are different, but there are many more.

Children Today

Here are some of the facts that make children different today:

1. *Family life.* Who is working? What values does the

family have? Our affluent society seems to be very much interested in *things*. Possession of material things as a family value is bound to influence the child.

2. *Modern necessities*. In this category we can put almost anything from the telephone to the garbage disposal. Each family finds its own values, but almost every American home has at least one TV—and probably a VCR, too. What a great influence this is on children. In mid-1972, advertisers attempted to develop a code for use on TV commercials viewed by children. One standard mentioned was, "Don't make parents look inferior." Had TV commercials made parents look inadequate? If so, some children naturally believed what they saw. Can you imagine your grandfather or great-grandfather being satisfied with an image that encouraged disrespect? As Sunday School teachers, we must be aware of the influence of TV. Some teachers have lost class attention by unwittingly using words or referring to characters dramatized on TV.

3. *Society's values*. Children are very sensitive to the values and ideas of others. Fads appear and disappear. Television links its cartoons to products through shows like *Care Bears* and *Masters of the Universe*. America aggressively markets the idea that boys and girls must have more and more things, and children learn to measure others by the possessions they have. Little girls of five must have pierced ears, and boys of seven have to wear the same shoes their classmates sport. While it's not our purpose to condemn or condone the cultural values children learn, we must be aware of the great impact of marketing and of other children's behavior on our boys and girls. And we need to realize that children's values today are not the same values that society maintained years ago.

4. *Public education.* The school reflects what is going on in society. It is an influence in children's lives because it is so definitely a large part of their lives. What they learn at school and the way they learn it influence children's values and attitudes—especially their attitudes toward the content of Sunday School lessons and the way they are taught. The Sunday School may never have the media available to the public school, but it should have available dedicated teachers who are teaching through the power of the Holy Spirit.

The old-fashioned picture of children was, "Kids will be kids—up to tricks, but innocent and fairly obedient." Many of today's children do not fit this picture. They look like children, but they act like adults. They have had various pressures put on them since the first grade. Their parents and teachers have expected them to be loving, respectful, well adjusted, poised, creative, and interesting. We have expected them to learn quickly, be eager to learn, and develop athletic or aesthetic abilities.

Because children are different in many ways from the way they were ten, fifteen, or twenty-five years ago, lists of age characteristics are not completely trustworthy. Lists of characteristics may give us some direction, but we must always be open to the fact that the unsophisticated first grader of our childhood has changed. First graders now are much more sophisticated, knowledgeable, and may have had experiences formerly reserved for high school students. If we were to draw up lists of characteristics applicable to children of this decade, how would they have to be changed to describe the children of the next? So we cannot stereotype children, but we do need to know them.

Understanding Development

Even though boys and girls are subject to many influences their parents were not, we need to be aware of their limitations. The content of children's thoughts and conversations may be different. But boys and girls still are not able to think and understand as adults.

Every normal person goes through a process in his or her development. In this process a child gradually becomes able to think and understand in more complex ways. Our teaching needs to be geared to the way a child thinks and understands, not the way adolescents or grown-ups think. The following list indicates some of the differences in thinking ability first identified by Jean Piaget. The list is adapted from my book, *A Theology of Children's Ministry* (Zondervan, 1983).

PIAGET'S STRUCTURAL STAGES

Preconceptual Stage (ages one and a half to four)

- ▶ imitative language, only partially understood
- ▶ objects seem stable, not able to grasp changing shapes due to perspective
- ▶ lacks abstracting ability to perceive space apart from perspective
- ▶ beginning to distinguish between past, present, and future
- ▶ reasoning is by analogy to experiences

Intuitive Stage (ages four to seven)

- ▶ language and thought still tied to phenomenal experience: words represent child's own experiences and perceptions (a bottle is "where you put water")
- ▶ comprehends and can respond to complex adult language, but does not understand such processes as conservation (the transfer of a principle or characteristic across situations)

- objects now maintain identity despite changes in position perspective
- number sense develops with ability to measure quantity
- can compensate fully for perspective changes caused by change in position
- time sense is still personalized, and interactions between time, distance, speed, etc., not grasped
- great interest in explaining causes of what is observed, understanding of causes still highly intuitive

Concrete Stage (ages seven to ten)

- can trace change in states through complex series rather than rely on impression of a particular observed state
- can take others' points of view and integrate their perspective with his or her own
- can begin to distinguish variables that cause change and mentally predict changes
- capacities to perceive objects, numbers, time, space all significantly developed
- mechanical explanations of cause are given priority (clouds move because the winds push)

Formal Operations Stage (ages ten to fifteen)

- only now does the ability to think about thought—to explore relations between the real and the possible—develop; "adult" kinds of thinking become possible

Awareness of the importance of development doesn't mean that a Sunday School teacher needs to have a degree in psychology. Good teachers have always been sensitive to boys and girls, and known intuitively how to communicate with them. But what we now know about development does mean two important things:

1. You need to use and rely on a good Sunday School curriculum. Curriculum writers should be specialists who understand human development, and who gear lesson content and method to the abilities of the age-group.

2. You need to take the time to come to know personally the children in your class. You need to listen to them, talk about the things that are important to them, become aware of their joys and their sorrows. There is no better way to be sure our teaching is truly geared to the level of the children we teach than to know our class members as individuals.

To understand children, a teacher must first have a genuine respect for them. We must accept children for what they are—accept them and want to help them. Then we need to recognize that each child is an individual and has an individual pattern of development. Wide differences exist among children at any age—another danger in confining ourselves to closely graded characteristics. A teacher cannot treat all children in a class in the same way! Some children need encouragement to participate, while others may need reminders from you to be cooperative, sharing materials and time.

Children develop as total persons. It is impossible to separate emotional, physical, mental, and spiritual growth. All processes go on at the same time.

Physical development during the first six years of life is most notable in size and maturity of bodily organs. Growth is fairly rapid in early childhood, slows down in middle childhood, and then accelerates again in adolescence.

Mental development usually means a child's understanding of words, symbols, and numbers. The wonderful world of reading opens many doors for the first grader who is eager to read. If there is a pattern of mental development about the concept of God, it would be that the younger child has questions about God and the older child has more understanding of who He is. But even this generalization is open to debate. We can also say that until the child is about ten years old, he or she cares much more about the present than about the future. Yet there will be exceptions to the generalization that young primaries are not as concerned about living forever with Jesus as is an older child.

Emotional development refers to the way a child grows in his or her attitude about something and learns to feel in various situations.

Social development is continuous and closely interwoven with physical, mental, and emotional development. As well as learning to accept society's values and grow in the role of a boy or girl, a child learns to be a member of various groups—home, church, school, and groups of boys and girls. As a child matures, he or she becomes more independent of adults. The young primary is very much concerned about the teacher's approval and tends to believe all that responsible adults tell him or her. The pattern changes as the child matures. Group opinion and approval become increasingly important.

A child does not automatically change on his or her birth date. Many children develop in similar ways, but there always are the early or late ones. It is impossible to discuss adequately the importance of Christian behavior at every age. Many publishers of Sunday School curriculum can furnish you with standards for attitudes and behavior anticipated at each age level.

Look at children patiently, repeatedly, respectfully, and hesitate in making judgments about them. Many teachers have a mental model of how a child should act. Hold on to your ideal, but be realistic in accepting the fact that your children are real children and may not resemble your model. You can learn to understand children through observing them, reading about them, even doing a case history on individual students; but most important, talk to them and listen to them talk to you.

Easily Identified Age Characteristics

Some generalizations can be made about children. But age characteristics given here are for guidance only. No list or chart can adequately describe the children you teach.

We can describe primaries (six-, seven-, and eight-year-olds) by saying that they are learning to read. The ability to read is very important to a learning child. Think about a lesson you have taught recently. What materials or methods would you have changed for nonreaders? Primaries have a literal, concrete world. Their reasoning power is limited, but their imaginations are still very active. Primaries are developing a sense of responsibility for their conduct. They need physical activity, and cannot help wiggling when they do not have it. They remember what they *do* more than what they see or hear. They believe what they are told. They have not had much experience in living, and therefore the present is very important to them.

We may describe juniors as doers. They are discovering the world! They are independent, active, and often boisterous. They do not seem to know fear. Juniors enjoy being members of a peer group and tend to be influenced more by the group than by adults. They like to think creatively, but need adult guidance. These children do not want to be dominated or over-directed. They are very critical of adults who tend to talk down to them, underestimate their abilities, or treat them "like babies." Juniors' ambitions often exceed their abilities. They may need a little help in keeping to realistic goals. They are growing in their sense of responsibility. Juniors are intensely concerned about justice. If a teacher does not seem fair, he or she is resented and criticized.

A teacher whose understanding of children is growing will remember that each child is in the process of becoming. The six-year-old is becoming a seven-year-old; the eleven-year-old is growing toward adolescence. Children do not remain in a state of suspension; they are constantly growing. There is a great difference between six-year-olds in the fall and the spring of the school year.

Talking to Children

There has been a great deal written on the self-concept. Perhaps a Sunday School teacher should think about the self-concept as he or she learns to talk with children and listen to them. Your conversations with children contribute to the feelings they have about themselves. In the past, educators, parents, and other adults significant to a child emphasized doing: do good work, work hard, be loyal, be brave, be truthful, and more. Recent thinking seems to center on being or the person: "Who am I?" "How do I feel about a situation, person, or object?" The Bible emphasizes a healthy balance. Christians can see themselves as persons God loves—total persons who are exhorted to serve Him. In teaching children, we must be aware of the current emphasis put on self and then lead them to see God's perfect balance.

What children do you want to talk with first,

remembering you want to discover a child's self-concept? Have you selected someone who is aggressive, boisterous, and a problem to you? Or have you chosen the quiet, shy, eager-to-please child who may not *be* a problem, but can *have* problems? What do you want to find out about the child?

- What does the child like or dislike?
- Who are his or her friends, heroes, or TV favorites?
- Who makes up the child's family?
- What pets does he or she have?
- What are some of the child's ideas about God?
- How does the child spend his or her free time?

Your conversation with children cannot resemble an interrogation. You should not approach a child with a list of questions and conduct an interview. Your job is to communicate—giving and receiving information and ideas. Conversation with children is not difficult if we remember to give them equal time. Sometimes an adult becomes uncomfortable if a child does not talk enough. Perhaps the child has not learned that he or she is expected to hold up one end of the conversation, an adult ability. Wait patiently for the child. If you are an adult the child likes and respects, he or she will talk when ready.

One of the aims in talking with children is to discover their beliefs, values, and even convictions. Conversation affords an excellent opportunity to help children who hold inaccurate spiritual concepts. Someone may sit in your class and seem to take in everything you say. But when you let that person express himself or herself in a casual way, you discover what he or she really thinks. For example, a teacher who stressed the perfection of Christ was stunned when she heard one of her six-year-olds say that he saw no use in trying to be obedient because Jesus was the only One who was good. Sometimes children have misunderstood the whole idea, sometimes a word or two has caused the problem, and sometimes we have not given them enough information. Conversation will help us discover what is wrong.

There is something else we should be aware of in talking with children. We are not preaching to them. We can clarify their concepts as we respond to them, but we should not be defensive. For example, the six-year-old's teacher could have responded, "But I never said that!" Instead, she listened patiently and then asked, "Dan, why do you think Jesus is perfect? Yes, because He is God's Son. Is anyone else God's Son? Can anyone else be just like Jesus? Do you think Jesus wants you to obey? Will He help you?" (Of course the teacher did not fire these questions one after another! She gave the child adequate time to respond.) As a result of their communication, the child decided he wanted to please Jesus by trying to be obedient.

Is there anything in the teacher's remarks to this child to show that she thought he was stupid? Was she defensive of her teaching? Did she lecture him? Did she criticize him? There are some clues here for every teacher who wants to talk with children and listen to them. After all, conversations with children which consist of criticism and instruction on one side and denials on the other have no place in the Sunday School room. Improving our ability to listen to children and talk with them is best attained through simply doing it. Experience will help you see your mistakes and not make them again. Remember that respect for the child and sincerity in talking with him or her are most important. Show understanding and respect for the child's feelings.

Our conversations with children should help them feel better about themselves. Often our conversations with children should revolve around a child's feelings—not the situation. The fact that a child has grabbed the scissors need not be discussed, but a teacher should say, "Did something make you feel that you had to have the scissors? How did you feel?" In responding to the feelings instead of the events, so psychologists tell us, a child may feel more comfortable. We all react to experiences, and it is our feelings that cause us concern. It was wrong of a neighbor to borrow something and not return it, but my feeling about the matter is much stronger than my loss of a small item! Children react in the same way; their feelings are more important than the event. If teachers can train themselves to remember this, conversation will be more effective.

It is not easy to feel free to discuss feelings with children. It takes practice. Keep in mind that you are serving as a mirror, reflecting the child's feelings through your remarks. This will help a child examine his or her feelings, deciding whether they are the attitudes he or she wants. What the Bible has to say about some of these feelings and acts may not be news to the child. Part of growing up is learning what is right and what is wrong. By the time a child reaches nine, ten, or eleven, he or she has a very good idea of what is acceptable behavior. Even the six-year-old recognizes his or her wrongdoing.

Many teachers would tell a child how he or she should feel, what the Bible says, and how wrong he or she is. The teacher would be right, but should not expect the child to be honest and free with him or her again! It is better to let a child decide what he or she wants to do about feelings.

Let's use the example of sibling rivalry—a natural experience. Is eight-year-old Michael, who expresses negative feelings about his sister Jenny, helped when a teacher says, "But Jesus doesn't want you to feel that way"? Michael knows that. He is already experiencing frustration and discomfort. But he is more likely to want to do something about his feelings if a sensitive teacher asks, "You think Jenny has things you wish you had?" After Michael answers, depending on how well the teacher knows the situation, he or she may say, "Does Jenny have a bike like yours?" The teacher will not continue, trying to draw an obvious conclusion. Leave that up to the child.

Once youngsters gain insight into their own emotions, they can begin to change those feelings. And they *can* change, with the Lord's help!

There is no simple formula to follow in listening to children and talking with them. But the following reminders may be helpful to you as you try this exciting way of learning to understand children:

1. Treat every child as an individual, with respect.
2. Be as sincere in talking with a child as you are with any of your friends.
3. Do not be impatient when a child does not talk. That child may enjoy and benefit from just being with you.
4. Do not be too quick to offer obvious answers. Children do not want answers any more than most adults do. They want a chance to try out what *they* think or feel.
5. Do not turn a child off with pat answers. For example, if a pet has died, a teacher might say, "You'll get another cat." True, but not a satisfying answer. The child wants to know that the teacher feels sorry with him or her and has some appreciation of what it is to

see the cold, hard, motionless body of a formerly playful pet. Do not be ashamed of your feelings or expect children to suppress theirs.

6. Balance your talking and listening time. A good rule for a teacher is to listen 75 percent of the time and talk 25 percent.

7. Evaluate your conversations afterward. Did you preach? Did your attitude express genuine interest? How did you help the child? What did you learn about him or her?

In understanding children, as in every other area of Christian living, we turn to the Lord Jesus. He, who knows the intent of every human heart and its needs, says, "If a man remains in me and I in him, he will bear much fruit; apart from me you can do nothing" (Jn. 15:5). Yes, the Lord promises fruit—Christian pupils growing in knowledge and behavior. But He also says we cannot produce this "fruit" without Him. Depend on Him to help you understand the boys and girls you teach!

REACT

1. In what ways do you think children today are different from when you were a child?

2. How do these differences affect the ministry of the Sunday School teacher?

ACT

1. Think of an experience you have had in listening to children. How has it helped you?

2. Decide when and how you can listen to the children in your class.

CHAPTER FOUR
HOW CHILDREN LEARN

▶ Recall the most meaningful learning experience you have ever had. What did you learn? How did you learn it? What factors entered into your learning: visual, audio, teacher, your own participation, or what?

Spend a little time recalling your personal experience, because doing so may help you answer the question, "How do children learn?" Now list a few of the factors that you think were important to your learning experience.

Which of these factors that helped you learn are evident in *your* teaching? Do you provide your pupils with the same learning environment that you found helpful?

If you have read the Successful Teaching Series, of which this book is one part, you may remember the following comments made in *Teachers: Teaching with Love*.

> *There are as many different meanings for the word* learning *as there are meanings for the word* teaching. . . . *Note the correspondence [in these examples]:*
>
> If teaching is—
> *causing to memorize the times tables,*
> *giving information about history,*
> *helping to develop driving skills,*

Then learning is—
memorizing the times tables,
mastering that information and demonstrating it on a test,
being able to drive.

But what is learning, if teaching is communicating God's Word as a reality that can be experienced? There can be only one answer: Learning is experiencing Bible truths!

How Do Children Experience Bible Truth?

The Christian teacher has some particulars to think about in a discussion of how children learn or experience Bible truth. He or she must consider:

That the definition of learning means experiencing abstract principles (Biblical truths) which are hard for a child to grasp.

That Bible stories, often the vehicle for teaching, describe events from a different culture and are difficult to present as reality.

That the whole atmosphere of Christian education has a right-wrong implication.

Most children want to be right—to do right, to give right answers, to be accepted as right-acting persons. This is fairly simple to illustrate in the secular sense. The date of the War of 1812 is 1812. If you know the date, you are right; there can be no argument.

But, asked to express an opinion on cheating, a child may be so concerned with the rightness-wrongness aspect that he or she is tempted to give the "right" answer even though he or she may personally think there are times when cheating is okay. Do you see how the right-wrong atmosphere may confuse a child and perhaps produce a sense of guilt in the child who has not given an honest answer?

Some religious educators look at these three factors,

plus some others, and conclude that the Bible is not for children. They are willing to teach only what they believe the child can understand: (1) Bible stories, often treated as fiction, told with no life relevancy; or (2) social action based on Biblical principles and equated with Christian living.

Because the true Christian teacher is committed to teaching the Bible as reality, he or she must make the Bible, God's Word, relevant to a child's life. The Bible can be relevant to a child's total life if the Christian teacher recognizes the role of the Holy Spirit in the teaching-learning process. There can be no real Bible teaching or learning without His supernatural work.

If true learning is experiencing Bible truth, we can never omit or minimize the vital function and relationship of the Holy Spirit with the individual teacher and pupil. A teacher must have a proper understanding of the function of the Word, the Spirit, *and* the teacher.

After teachers recognize the role of the Holy Spirit, they can turn to the areas they can influence—choosing passages from the Bible to teach, and preparing for teaching. If they understand how children think, teachers will better understand how they must prepare.

What Are 'Levels of Learning'?

Learning generally follows the natural growth patterns and develops with some regard to these factors:

1. *Physical development.* The child's ability to learn improves with age.

2. *Necessity.* There must be a reason for learning a particular subject. Young parents need to learn how to raise their children. Senior citizens need to learn how to live on their retirement income.

3. *Opportunity.* How will the person use what he or

she learns? Much learning seems to be lost through disuse. Why should a student remember Greek, for example, if he or she never reads or writes in that language?

Keeping in mind that learning follows the natural growth pattern, let's look at some stages of growth or development. Jean Piaget, child psychologist and author of many books on child development, defines four levels of learning that are especially helpful to Sunday School teachers. Here are expanded descriptions of these stages, which were introduced in Chapter 3.

1. *Sensory-motor period (birth to about two years of age)*

The baby is taking in the environment. He or she hears, smells, and manipulates objects in order to develop. The touch-hear-see method of learning continues throughout childhood, but in early years it is a child's chief means of learning.

Recognition of this level of development helps teachers understand why young children must be permitted to touch and feel. It is futile to bring objects into the Nursery Department of the Sunday School and expect the children to appreciate looking at what they cannot hold.

Children in the years between six and eleven will continue to want to feel. Give any child a smooth plastic object, a rough, hairy surface, or a wind chime, and you will see immediately that he or she is still learning through the senses.

2. *Preoperational thought—(two to seven years)*

The child is not able to use certain mental operations which are necessary for mature reasoning and understanding. He or she can classify or categorize but uses only one attribute at a time. It is hard for a child of this age to understand that an object has many properties.

Perhaps the most easily illustrated example is found in the pupil-teacher relationship. A child comes to expect a teacher to act like a teacher at all times. The child associates the teacher with the classroom or church building. When a young child meets a teacher in a store or at a sports event, he or she may register surprise—not realizing that a teacher is also a human being who enjoys sports or buys food at a store.

Another example may be seen in the child's understanding of God. "God is everywhere; He is with me in church." But it takes a teacher to help a child realize that he or she can say, "God is with me everywhere; He is with me when I'm in the bathtub (or on my bike, etc.)."

A child at this stage also makes judgments in terms of how things look to him or her rather than on the basis of a mental operation. Again an illustration from the Sunday School room: Show a child a picture of a missionary which is larger than a map illustrating the country where the missionary works. You may be greeted with laughter. Why? If the child gives you an answer it may be, "How can that man work in a place that isn't as big as he is? Look, he's bigger than Africa."

During this period, a child is very dependent on appearances. Pour red liquid into a cup measure. Then pour the same liquid into a tall, slender vase. The child will tell you there is more liquid in the vase than in the cup. The preoperational period is a factor in the way children think and in the ways we teach them.

3. *Concrete operations—(seven to ten or eleven years)*

The child becomes able to manipulate data mentally.

He or she can come to logical conclusions, define, compare, and contrast. The child is capable of logical thought, and no longer trusts only the senses to teach him or her.

This stage of development seems to be a big step, but it also has its limitations. Remember the word *concrete.* A child thinks concretely at this stage. Things must seem logical in a very concrete way. To tell a child at this stage that an unconverted sinner is like a pig wallowing in the mud makes little sense. The child's conclusion may be that sin is mud and a sinner is a pig. Do not think this is an exaggeration!

After hearing an object lesson in which a Christian was said to be like a boat whose cargo of sin had been tossed overboard, a nine-year-old said, "I never knew Jesus put my sins in a bag and took them down to the bottom of the ocean." Entirely too many stories have been told about children's misinterpretations of Biblical passages and phrases from old hymns for one to remain unmoved or unbelieving. Unfortunately, many object lessons, chalk-talks, and messages for children count on a child's being able to think abstractly.

4. *Formal operations—(about eleven or twelve)*

In this last period defined by Piaget, a child can think in abstract terms. He or she can foresee results. It is at this time that religious symbolism begins to have meaning. Juniors who are at this stage of development like to prepare their own visual interpretations of Scripture. "Blessed is the man who does not walk in the counsel of the wicked. He is like a tree planted by streams of water. Not so the wicked! They are like chaff that the wind blows away" (Ps. 1:1,3,4) has real meaning for the ten-or eleven-year-old. These children can be introduced to the beauty of some of the figurative language used in the Bible.

This very simple explanation of Piaget's stage theory of development may help teachers understand the mistakes children can make in their reasoning. A teacher cannot expect a child to understand Bible truth when the child does not have the ability to receive it. There are no shortcuts in teaching logical thinking.

Curriculum writers are aware of a child's limitations and select Scripture that children can receive at the various stages of development in their thinking. But because Christian teachers deal with such important truths and are eager to have children know more of the Bible, they often do not realize how much or how little an individual child understands. It is always easy to mistake a child's saying the right words for genuine understanding. And children can deliver the right answers without actually knowing the meaning of the words they are using. Teachers and parents must listen to children to know what they can and cannot understand.

What Is Planned Learning?

Reasoning in children from ages seven to ten or eleven is based mostly on observation. Not until a child is about eleven is he or she able to make abstract assumptions. Before that time, a child is learning through methods of teaching that involve one physically: creative writing, drawing, roleplaying, looking at visuals, listening to records, tapes, and cassettes, and problem solving in situations where he or she may have had experience. The more a child experiences through actual participation, the less danger there will be of misunderstanding. A pupil must be personally involved for true learning to take place.

Learning is experiencing Bible truths, and includes:

Knowing—intellectual knowledge of facts and the

ability to repeat them. The following type of Sunday School information falls into this category: memory verses and references, books of the Bible, names of characters, geographical locations, and chronological events.

Feeling—emotional experience. In current vogue is the idea, "I know deeply only that which I feel deeply." Feeling is important in responding to God's Word, but it must not be substituted for the facts of His Word.

Doing—desired results. Much learning takes place through doing. Doing, responding, or acting upon should be the end result of learning, but it is also a means of learning. A young child learns to write by writing, just as he or she acquires other skills.

Scripture lays great emphasis on the knowledge of God and His truth. Knowledge is basic to doing and experiencing. Whereas penmanship may be a purely mechanical skill, a child discovers spiritual truth when he or she learns to pray by praying. The child's discovery of spiritual truth is based on a growing knowledge of and personal relationship with God. The child learning penmanship uses fingers and brain, but the child learning to pray is involved as a total person, using brain, emotions, and the physical skill of speaking a prayer.

But even though any statement about learning must acknowledge knowing, feeling, and doing, Christian education must recognize that the end result of learning is change and growth—application to life. Spiritual growth occurs through changes in attitudes, emotional responses, and behavior or action. Maturity as a Christian occurs only as a person puts off the sinful nature and moves into new life with God in Christ Jesus. Christian education deals with more than facts or feelings; its goal is to change the individual. What outline, formula, or lesson plan will help a teacher teach so that this kind of learning takes place?

The four-step plan described in the following paragraphs will work! It is easy to remember, is purposeful, includes both knowing and feeling, and leads the pupil to do—through action or attitude. This plan is usable with children, adolescents, and adults, and is incorporated in many contemporary Sunday School curriculums. Study the plan until you understand how the four parts can apply to any lesson that is meant to teach the Bible's reality and relevance to the life of the student. Do not think of these four parts as mechanical steps. They are four parts of a *continuous* process.

The methods for setting the "hook," guiding pupils to the Bible, helping them look at the implications of Bible truth for themselves, and experiencing Bible truth will be discussed in other chapters. Only the basic principle is outlined here to demonstrate how it relates to children's learning.

1. The HOOK gets the students into the lesson. The hook is a teacher's tool. Sometimes the hook raises a question or sets a goal. It defines a life need, leading pupils to explore Bible content for the answer.

2. The BOOK provides the answer. After a teacher has "hooked" the pupil, the pupil begins to ask the questions. The pupil is ready to discover the answer as the teacher communicates Biblical information in understandable form. This is Bible learning.

3. The LOOK helps a pupil see personal implications. As the pupil hears, understands, and accepts Bible truth, he or she must decide what to do about it. He or she is asking the question, "What does this mean

for me?" and seeing how truth understood relates to life. He or she is making a Bible application.

4. The TOOK, or life response, helps a pupil act on what he or she has learned. After the pupil realizes the personal implications of Bible truth, he or she is ready to assume responsibility to carry truth into his or her life. He or she is ready to do, to respond, to act on what has been heard, understood, and accepted. Depending on the pupil's maturity, he or she may be able to apply Bible truth in many situations.

What Motivation Can We Give Children to Learn?
Many teachers think this is a difficult question. Actually, it is not. What do you want children to learn? The way you motivate them depends on what you want them to know. Are you interested in pupils' growing relationship to God? Or in the large number of facts they know? If the latter question expresses your aim, then a reward system of some sort may be important to your children.

However, if you want children to grow in their own relationship to the Lord, then you are one of the best motivators. What is your relationship to the Lord? Is your example one of living faith—a daily, exciting experience with the Lord? Can you regularly report to your students the Lord's work in your own life? Can you say that you are merely a human through which the Holy Spirit works?

A second motivator is pupil needs. Are you teaching pupils or lessons? If you are teaching pupils, you are working week by week to help them personally experience Bible truth. If you are teaching lessons, not pupils, then needs are not so important and you are not using them for motivation to discover Bible truth.

One easy way to motivate children is to stress the love or fear of God. In Christianity, the motivation to learn can be fear of separation from God or a desire to know God—either fear or love. Which are you using? Which should you be using?

What should children learn about the Christian life? Children should, after receiving Jesus Christ as Savior, grow up to be mature Christians, the kind of people God wants them to be. This growth is possibly only through the work of the Holy Spirit.

But responsible, dedicated adults can work *with* the Holy Spirit when they understand the goal of learning, how children learn, planned learning, and motivation.

REACT

1. If children learn more through active participation then passive observation, what can a teacher do?
2. If you accept Piaget's stages of development, what application does it have to your class? Where do you think your pupils are?

ACT

1. Think about your own experiences in teaching and learning. Now look at the four-step teaching plan described in this chapter. Can you see that your most effective teaching involved all or some of the four steps?

2. If you are currently teaching, look over the next lesson you will present to your children. Decide how you can include any or all of the four steps.

CHAPTER FIVE
GROUPING CHILDREN

▶The Lord Jesus taught the multitudes (Mk. 6:34). He taught the small group of twelve (Mk. 3:13, 14). He also taught the individual—Peter, in this instance (Mt. 18:21).

There are times when we teach the "multitudes," the large group, such as a department. The individual Sunday School teacher works with the small group, the class, or counsels the individual student. We vary our teaching according to the number of pupils, available teachers, and the facilities. But how do we determine who should be in the large group and who should be in the small group? And what is the difference between grouping and grading?

Grouping usually means combining in one group the children of particular ages who are in specific grades in public school. Grading, on the other hand, may mean setting up qualifications for an individual to meet in order to belong to a particular group. Very little grading of this sort is being done in the Sunday School. In this chapter the two words will be used interchangeably.

When we group children in any particular way, we

are considering how many children are enrolled, what we want to accomplish, what space and facilities for teaching are available, and how many potential teachers can be put to work. All of these factors relate to one another and cannot be regarded separately. A Sunday School could have an enrollment of 195 and 50 teachers, but space for only 20 classes.

What is an ideal number for a class or for a department? When are there too many children in a department? Deciding when a department has too many is not necessarily dependent on space. For example, a Primary Department may be meeting in the church sanctuary. Three hundred boys and girls sit in pews across the width of the church. Is this too many? There is still room for more. Yes, it is too many—because not all the children can see the visuals, have eye contact with the teacher in charge, or even participate. If you were an eight-year-old boy in the last row and no teacher were near you, would you be more interested in learning Bible verses or in talking to the person next to you?

In this book we are dealing with children of public school age, grades one through six. Do they all belong in one department? Are two departments enough? How many classes are necessary?

In organizing by age or school grade, we are assuming that children of the same age or grade are more likely to have similar interests, needs, and abilities than children of different grades or ages would. This is not always true. Some experimental grouping of children with similar interests has been done in public schools. In one school, all children interested in astronomy have been placed together, thus including children of all ages. These interest-group combinations may work in public schools because there are specially trained teachers and plenty of materials—books, models, films, and so on. At the present it seems impractical to suggest interest combinations for the Sunday School.

You can begin to determine grouping for your own Sunday School by writing down your enrollment in each of the following categories:

First graders (six-year-olds)
Second graders (seven-year-olds)
Total number of children in first and second grades

Third graders (eight-year-olds)
Fourth graders (nine-year-olds)
Total number of children in third and fourth grades

Fifth graders (ten-year-olds)
Six graders (eleven-year-olds)
Total number of children in fifth and sixth grades

Total number of children in first through sixth grades

Now that you have ascertained the number of pupils—or potential pupils—for your Sunday School, look at the next list. This represents the ideal situation toward which you want to work:

Number of pupils in grade	Number of classes
3-20	1-4
21-40	4-5
41-100	5-16

A Sunday School with less than three children in any one grade of public school would combine more than one age to form a class. Children who are ages six or seven would be placed together in a primary class. Children who are eight or nine would be placed together in a primary-junior class. Children who are ten or eleven should be placed together in a junior class. Then, when either class grows to more than eight children, it should be divided to make two classes. Holding the class size to no more than five to seven, the superintendent will continue to form classes as more children attend. As soon as there are three children of the same age or grade in public school, they will be placed together in one class.

Be sure to place children in the Sunday School class or group that corresponds to their school grade. For example, if a child is seven years old, but just beginning first grade, keep him or her in the first grade class, even though other children are only six years old. What should you do about the child who fails in public school? It is usually better to keep him or her in the same grade at Sunday School. You may want to move the child on to the next class, but he or she should not be promoted to the next department. A sixth grader is lost emotionally, socially, and sometimes mentally when promoted into the Junior High department. Talk with the child and his or her parents, reaching a solution that is agreeable to them.

How will you form departments? Follow the numerical formula given in the following list:

Total pupils, grades 1-2 or 3-4 or 5-6	Number of departments
9-45	1
46-90	2
91-120	3
121-160	4

When you have nine or more children in first and second grades, or third and fourth grades, or fifth and sixth grades, organize a department. The first two grades are called the Primary Department. The middle two grades are the Primary-Junior Department, and the last two are the Junior Department. If you have a middle school system in your public or Christian day school, rearrange these groupings to fit the situation most familiar to your students. A sixth grader in middle school, for example, may feel too old to be called a junior in Sunday School.

Departments should not become so large that the children lose out in participation and attention from leaders. Ideally, a department will have 25 to 35 children, but no more than 50. When you have 20 or more children of one age or public school grade, consider organizing this group into a separate department. In a large church, these may be designated Primary 1 and Primary 2. The same organization is followed with the other grades.

As a general rule, small classes—five to eight children—are ideal. In a small group a pupil feels that he or she belongs. The teacher is able to sense the needs of each individual and to use teaching methods that involve every child. Teachers find it easier to maintain eye contact and hold the interest of every child. The small group is important if children are to receive and live Bible truth.

When should all the primary, primary-junior, and junior classes meet together as a department? This is up to the individual church to decide. They might meet every week for specific learning or worship experiences, preceding or following Bible study by classes. Here are some of the reasons for meeting as a department:

1. To participate in corporate worship, including singing and other large group activities.

2. To feel a part of the larger mission of the Sunday School—the body of believers. Primaries, primary-juniors, and juniors enjoy being a part of "the Lord's army," along with older children and adults.
3. A "master teacher," which the department superintendent often is, has an opportunity to teach all the children.
4. Announcements are made and the offering received, conserving class time. (Meeting together should never be a way of using up time. Some churches may decide to use this time for individual classes. We'll look at that later in this chapter.)

"What If We Can't Reach the Ideal?"

Perhaps you have already said, "But we can't!" in reacting to the number of pupils suggested for classes and departments. Maybe you cannot manage it right away, but you can work toward the ideal. There is no situation so impossible that it cannot be improved in some way.

If you cannot enlist enough workers now, use the ideal situation as your goal. In the meantime, try training high school students to teach in the Primary Department. High school young people who are dedicated to the Lord can become very capable teachers. They must be trained, supported in prayer, and encouraged by the rest of the teaching staff. Make sure these teens still have a time when they are studying the Bible at their own level.

Team teaching is one way to use fewer teachers, though no more than 40 children should be taught as a group. Team teaching does mean more teachers' meetings and requires better communication among teachers. The main way in which team teaching differs from other forms of teaching is the group planning that teachers must do.

In team teaching, the teachers in a department meet together weekly to discuss the aims, content, and methods for a lesson. As a team, the teachers examine the material, discuss how to teach, and decide who should assume responsibility. One teacher may tell the Bible story, another teach a song, a third show a short video that emphasizes the lesson aim. The teachers plan together and then share responsibility. In this way, two or three teachers could work with a group of 40 children. However, team teaching is not merely alternating responsibility. It should be team planning to allow each teacher to participate in the way best suited to his or her abilities. Each team teaching session should be evaluated, teachers being willing to accept criticism in order to improve. The chief value of team teaching is that fewer teachers are needed, each teacher will be doing what he or she can do best, and the children can all see or hear the available audio-visual teaching aids.

If team teaching is used in the elementary departments, every possible effort should be made to enlist parents for small group discussion. The large group may worship together and participate in the Bible study, but some opportunity should be provided for children to gather in small groups to discuss Bible content and application. This discussion may center around the pupils' workbooks, a team teacher may suggest questions for discussion, or the pupils themselves may be encouraged to suggest questions. Review again the "HOOK-BOOK-LOOK-TOOK" steps in Chapter 4. The group discussion must involve the last step, if learning is to carry over into life.

Some Sunday Schools' departments follow another

method of varying groups. The Sunday School hour is divided into several periods. One or more teachers are in charge of each period, and the children rotate from one teacher to another. For example, a third of the juniors may be engaged in Bible activities, another third may be studying the Bible, and the remaining third participating in worship. This is a solution to teacher shortage, but it is not ideal. While some juniors may be able to move from Bible activities—perhaps the HOOK in the four-step process—to Bible study, and culminate in worship, other juniors must begin with the Bible study or worship. Only a third of the total number of juniors can experience the "HOOK-BOOK-LOOK-TOOK" steps that have proved so important in understanding Bible truth.

Two other ways of grouping should be discussed, though they are not solutions to the teacher shortage problem. Both extended sessions and individualized instruction require more teacher preparation, but provide additional learning for the children.

There is a great need for extended sessions in Sunday School. If you have read *Teaching with Love*, another book in this Successful Teaching Series, you have discovered how much one teacher accomplished by spending more time with her pupils. Still, the program must be planned; this is not an invitation to waste time! But when we see what children should learn, we realize how very much time we need to share and interact with our pupils.

Ideally, children should have two and a half to three hours in an uninterrupted block of time. In the average 45 minutes allotted to Sunday School, children cannot share in any enriching activities that would help them relate Bible truth to themselves. In the usual class situation, the teacher does the relating. For example, when children have time to draw a map and locate places, they are really learning Bible background. When children have an opportunity to make a "helping" scrapbook or illustrate "Trusting God when I am afraid," they are applying Bible truth to themselves—to their own lives and current experiences.

In the extended session, children have opportunity to make visuals—not merely see them. They can record on tape—not just listen. They can participate in skits or roleplay or record themselves on video, actually feeling the perspectives and attitudes of various characters. The extended session is still a pioneer movement, but it is an important direction for teachers to consider.

Many churches call the second portion of this time Children's Church. Children participate in a worship service at their own level and receive training that allows them to be active participants when they enter the adult worship.

Individualized instruction is almost an unexplored area in Christian education. It is work, but it is worth it. Projects, assignments, extra reading, assisting the teacher at home or in class, and preparing teaching aids are all ways of helping the individual pupil work at his or her top capacity.

Sunday School teachers must also know how their pupils are being taught in public school and adapt their teaching accordingly. If pupils spend five days a week discovering their own answers, they find it hard to spend an hour once a week as silent listeners.

What About Facilities and Equipment?

The space you need and the furniture for it depend on the number of classes and departments in your Sunday School. Ideally, every department will have room for the children to meet together and space to meet in small groups. The usual pattern is a large department room and small classrooms. Chairs should be comfortable for the pupils. Juniors can usually adjust to adult-size chairs, but primaries should have child-sized, or juvenile, furniture.

Teachers will want writing space for their pupils. This may be a table around which the class can gather. However, lapboards can be used. If primaries must meet in the church sanctuary, they can kneel in front of the pews to do their writing. If possible, juniors will enjoy having chairs with a desk arm.

Yes, the facilities also "teach." Children who are accustomed to attractive homes expect to find the same care given to the church. Disorderly or neglected rooms give a child a negative attitude toward the importance of Bible truth.

In arranging any room, consider the relationship of the teacher to the pupils and the pupils to one another—and the content that is to be presented. Vary the room arrangement. Some children enjoy sitting in rows; others like circles. If you want to promote worship in a more formal situation, arrange the chairs in rows, but not straight rows. Arrange them in semicircular rows, giving a feeling of warmth and fellowship. In the small group, try to arrange the chairs in a circle or hollow square if each one has a desk, or around the table. If the teacher sits with the children in both the large group time and small class, he or she will establish better rapport with the pupils. Physical closeness can develop an atmosphere of Christian fellowship and makes the teacher "a real person."

New Goals for the Sunday School

Throughout the history of the "big-little school," as the

Sunday School has been called, a great deal of spiritual ground has been gained. However, there is more to do, and grouping and grading offer fresh challenges.

At present, pupils are promoted in the Sunday School as they attain a particular grade in public school. It would be impossible not to promote a pupil in the present structure of the Sunday School. What effect does this attitude toward promotion have on the child?

How does the child's attitude toward Sunday School differ from his or her attitude toward public school? Most children do not consider Sunday School a real school or an educational experience, because both teachers and parents have made children feel this way. Parents are not nearly as concerned with either Sunday School curriculum or attendance as they are with public school subjects and their child's daily presence. One of the new goals for the Sunday School should be to help parents feel the importance of home and church working together to communicate Bible truth into pupils' experience. For help in this area, see another book in this Successful Teaching Series, entitled, *Parents: Round-the-Clock Teachers*.

Should the local Sunday School decide that there is particular Bible knowledge a child should have by the time he or she is in third grade or sixth grade? Should Sunday School teachers work with the home to help children gain this specific knowledge? Should a teacher invite a pupil home for special tutoring sessions? Bible truths must be lived or experienced, but it is also true that a certain amount of factual Bible knowledge helps a child see the Bible as reality.

If the Sunday School were to insist on attainment of knowledge goals instead of automatic promotion, there would be some resistance. Teachers would have to be trained to evaluate their teaching, to measure pupils' factual Bible knowledge, and to improve their methods. Parents and pupils would need to accept this new idea: There are definite knowledge goals to be attained in the Christian education program.

This idea may be new to you. In view of other immediate goals your Sunday School has, it may not seem important. But it is worthwhile to ask yourself, "Am I ready to become involved in a program like that? Do I have measurable goals? What do I really expect my pupils to know?"

To move a step further, ask yourself whether you want promotion to hinge entirely on content goals. For example, what about the child who can't recite the names of the 12 disciples—but knows how to live as a disciple of Jesus at school? Measuring the whole fabric of a child's life is a many-threaded issue!

REACT

1. How does your Sunday School measure up to some of the standards set in this chapter?
2. In which area does more work need to be done in your Sunday School—organization, establishment of teachers, training of teachers, arrangement of space and equipment, or establishing knowledge goals?

ACT

1. Choose one new idea that has come to you through this chapter. What can you do about it?
2. Plan to take one constructive step this week to reach your goal.

CHAPTER SIX
COMMUNICATING GOD'S WORD

►"All Scripture is God-breathed and is useful for teaching, rebuking, correcting and training in righteousness, so that the man of God may be thoroughly equipped for every good work" (II Tim. 3:16, 17).

The Bible is God's Guidebook! What a disservice we do children when we pass the Bible on to them as mere advice—not making God's revelation reality for them.. The Bible is one means whereby children can meet God—not just learn about Him!

To make plain the reality of the Bible, we need to take a very literal approach to it. The Bible *is* reality! Too often young people seem to think that the Word of God needs to be explained in the light of modern science or psychology or education. The Bible is the inerrant Word of God and is applicable to a person of any age. Current theories, though given new names, are not very different from old theories; situational ethics and the "existential moment" have had their counterparts in history. Nor is there any explanation for what the Bible has done in the lives of people who take it literally, except that the Bible is the Word of God.

Even though many passages in the Bible are beyond

the understanding of elementary school children, God has something to say to children from His Word. It is our job as teachers to communicate what He is telling them. The Lord uses human teachers and His Holy Spirit to cause life to spring up in the hearts of our pupils as the Bible is taught. God has promised that His Word will accomplish what He wants it to do (Isa. 55:11), and He has been pleased to use teachers in sending forth His Word.

A teacher who leads a child into the Bible is not using just another resource. He or she is bringing that child into the presence of the Author. For this encounter with God to have lasting value, however, the pupil must do more than mentally understand the Word. His or her head knowledge must change to heart response! The pupil must hear God speaking to him or her from His Word. And as soon as possible, a child should know that God's Word contains things God wants people to know. The Bible has science in it, but it is not a science book. The Bible gives many place names and history, but it is not a geography or a history book. The Bible has thrilling episodes, but it is not a storybook. The Bible is the Word of God, containing exactly what God wants to reveal about Himself.

The Bible teaching a child receives should relate to the child's present needs and experiences. The primary value of Bible teaching is not to instill ideas which students will need to know someday; the goal is to bring pupils into vital relationship with God *now!*

If you are following a Sunday School curriculum, you are probably teaching the parts of the Bible that trained Christian educators believe to be suitable for the age you are teaching. Because many curriculum writers have spent years in training and are constantly researching educational methods, you should generally feel secure in accepting their lesson outlines. You will take these "blueprints" and adapt them as necessary to meet the needs of your children.

A few words of caution may be helpful. Be sure that the curriculum holds the Word of God as the ultimate authority. Watch that the Bible stories do not read into the Bible ideas that are not there. It is not God's purpose to glorify man, though Hebrews 11 certainly recognizes the faith of individuals. Some curriculum writers tend to make Bible characters more noble than the Biblical accounts do. For example, is it the power of Christ or the generosity of the boy with the loaves and fishes that made possible the feeding of the 5,000? Is it Dorcas's unusual kindness, that she was following the standards set by early believers, or God's power that should be emphasized, in her life and return from the dead? Be sure you are not taking incidents out of their context and giving them meaning they were not meant to communicate.

The teacher wants to teach the Bible as reality, but is that all he or she will teach? No, there will be other material:

- How was the Bible put together?
- Who are the people in the Bible?
- Who have been some of the great Christians of the past? (Church history can be taught in elementary form to juniors.)
- What are the great hymns of the Church saying to us?
- Who are some of the people God has used? (Missionary heroes and denominational leaders have a contribution to make to the lives of boys and girls.)
- What do we need to know about God, salvation, sin, people, and the world?

Do not let the material in the preceding list overwhelm you. If you are following an adequate curriculum, much of this information has already been written into the lessons for you. The purpose of this chapter is to make you aware of what you are teaching and why.

First of all, your course of study should be organized by units or topics. A unit is a series of lessons centered on one theme and purpose. Every lesson in the unit expands on the central theme and contributes to the purpose of the unit. Unit teaching means that lessons are related to and build on one another. Look over your teaching resources to see how they will help you teach by units.

Why Must I Teach Bible Facts?

Bible facts must be the framework for perceiving Bible truth. This chapter may help you see why teachers should teach both Bible facts and truth. Keep in mind that Bible truth is a generalization developed through knowing a number of facts. For example, Jesus said, "Love each other as I have loved you" (Jn. 15:12). This is Bible truth. The Bible facts, in this instance, describe how Jesus washed His disciples' feet, proving His love.

Some Christian educators once emphasized teaching Bible truth almost to the exclusion of Bible facts. But a child must have Bible facts to understand Bible truths. For example, unless children know what it cost Abram to obey God, they do not have as deep an appreciation for the patriarch's obedience. When they know what cultural standards existed in Ur, how desolate and unknown the trip was likely to be, and how difficult it might be for Abram in the new land, they better understand what obedience to God really meant. The apostle Paul can serve as another illustration of obedience. When a junior knows something of Jewish custom and Greek culture, he or she can appreciate Paul's obedience. It may not have been an easy task for Paul to go to Troas, home of the famous Trojans!

When people say we should not teach Bible facts, they overlook a basic truth: an accurate and intelligent understanding of what the Bible says must be based on the facts that the Bible gives. This does not mean *unrelated* facts, however. There are games and books that quiz the reader on completely unrelated facts: How many disciples? How many chapters in Isaiah? How long did Abram spend in Haran? Who was Moses' mother? These facts do not build on one another. They do not contribute to any particular Bible truth or understanding relevant to life today. Knowledge of unrelated facts is proof of a teacher's ability to drill, a student's photographic memory, or the emphasis of a workbook that majors on meaningless questions.

Related facts, on the other hand, will contribute to a child's total understanding of a Bible truth. Let's look at an example, using the HOOK-BOOK-LOOK-TOOK steps introduced in Chapter 4. The Bible lesson is about the unforgiving servant (Mt. 18:21-35). Most juniors know they are supposed to forgive others, but how can we bring them to the point of really encountering God so that they will want to forgive? How do the four learning steps apply? Here are things you might say to juniors in such a class:

HOOK: Can you think of a time when it was hard for your parents to forgive you? What was the hardest time for you to forgive someone else? (Let the children talk about the experiences they recall. You are dealing with the child's life need.)

BOOK: Once the disciples had a hard question about forgiveness. Peter asked Jesus, "How many times shall

I forgive my brother when he sins against me? Up to seven times?" Why do you think the disciples asked this question? Let's get into Bible learning and read how Jesus answered them. (The children discover from the Bible passage that a person who has been forgiven should forgive others "from your heart.")

LOOK: Let's make a list of times when parents need to remember to forgive. Let's make another list of times boys and girls your age need to forgive. What an important Bible application!

TOOK: Tell us about something that will probably make you upset this week, and tell us how you're going to forgive the person because Jesus forgives you. This is life response.

Look again at the brief and simple outline to decide where Bible facts are important. Of course it will be in the BOOK area. Unless these juniors understand the enormity of the unforgiving servant's act, they will miss a vital part of the lesson. The verses in Matthew show more than "some guy who wouldn't forgive his servant." But until a teacher takes time to do some digging, to direct pupils to Bible facts, and to place the entire event in a Biblical setting, he or she has not taught the lesson. Facts are needed. When pupils understand the facts, they can come to the same conclusion: Forgiving is really a big thing. As a teacher might summarize, "It is not always an easy thing to do, but when I love the Lord enough I can say, 'Lord, I don't feel like forgiving him. He really did cheat me. But because I love You so much, help me to forgive him.' "

If we overlook the necessity of related Bible facts, we may be missing one other very important point. If children don't learn the facts undergirding Bible doctrines, how will they believe and defend those truths when doubts come?

What kind of facts are we talking about? Related facts—those with meaning, those that help us understand and interpret Bible events. When deciding which facts to minimize and which to emphasize, look at the lesson through the eyes of your pupils. What will the facts mean to them? Do they really need to know how many horses, bushels of grain, or head of cattle King Solomon had? What do you need to tell them to impress them with King Solomon's wealth and power? Would the foreign visitors who came to see him mean more? Remember, the facts you include must serve a definite purpose.

How Do Facts Build Concepts?

Sunday School teachers are helping pupils form concepts about God, man, sin, salvation, and the world. These concepts should be formed on the basis of Bible facts—what God says. Naturally, the Bible does not have one single chapter on any one of these concepts. But throughout the Bible, one related fact after another helps to shape a child's understanding of basic concepts.

As children study the Bible, they are likely to go over the same event many times. If they see the event only as a Bible story heard before, they become frustrated. But if they learn more from the event as they review it at succeeding age levels, they enlarge their concepts. For example, the first time a child hears the story of baby Moses, he or she may recognize God's care. However, when a junior begins to sense the way God kept His people in Egypt, providing a deliverer in Moses, instructing Moses in the desert, and sending him to face Pharaoh, the baby in the basket becomes one event among all the incidents that are helping this junior form his or her concept of God's omniscience and omnipotence.

The knowledgeable teacher can see that the facts of the event help to shape a child's concept. While a child will not have an understanding of the Lord's relationship to his or her life as an adult may have, the child will have a meaningful understanding of God's care and protection of him or her.

The most important concept, belief, or understanding you want children to have concerns their personal salvation. Unless children know Christ as Savior, their Bible knowledge is only intellectual attainment. When children know Christ as Savior, Bible knowledge helps them live as God's children. A child's response to an invitation for salvation is discussed in Chapter 9 of this book. Salvation is so important that it needs more consideration than can be given to it in this chapter.

Must Children Memorize Scripture?

Many teachers ask this question, and the answer can be, "No, you don't need to ask children to memorize Scripture. It's a lot of work! Besides, isn't there a Bible verse that reads, 'Thy Word have I hid in my heart until I was 12 years old'?"

Many adults seem to think there is such a verse; at least they do not memorize Scripture. Perhaps they are not under pressure to do so, and the rewards are not high enough. After all, what adult wants a gold star, a Bible puzzle, or a pencil with a verse on it? These and other rewards, including plastic trophies, may be sufficient to motivate children, but they are not large enough rewards for the adult.

Perhaps you ask, "But are kids supposed to memorize for rewards?" No, they surely are not to memorize for rewards. If we use rewards as a means of motivation, we indicate that the Bible verses are not really very meaningful; they are not worth learning for their own value.

If adults do not memorize Scripture and kids are not supposed to be rewarded, what should we do about Bible memory work? First of all, teachers should realize why it is hard to get children to memorize. Then teachers must decide what parts of the Bible should be memorized and how children can be helped to memorize.

Because of the great quantity of printed material available, there is less need or motivation to memorize. Less than 200 years ago, the average North American or European may have had only a few books to call his or her own. Today it is easy for most in our culture to have several shelves of books. There is more printed material being produced than ever before. And public school educators seem to consider it more important to read for knowledge than to memorize. For example, the grade school student is asked to read many books on a topic. In the past, students spent less time in reading and more time in learning poetry such as Longfellow's "Hiawatha" or Kipling's "Recessional."

Also, many children of nine, ten, or eleven expect the computer to recall any information they need. They do not see the necessity for memorizing facts or formulas. "And," they ask, "as long as everyone has a Bible, why bother to learn chapters from it?"

Another reason why Scripture memorizing is not being emphasized in the Sunday School is the multiplicity of versions. Next time you face a Sunday School class of juniors who have brought Bibles, ask how many have the King James Version. You may discover four or five different versions represented in a group of 20 children. The variety of versions is a handicap when it comes to group memorization of Bible portions.

However, along with all the reasons given for not memorizing Scripture, we can find several good reasons *for* memorizing. In addition to challenging children to commit helpful passages to memory, we should be able to show them the value of memorizing Scripture.

Any young child can see how confusing it would be if he or she never memorized his or her telephone number or address. A creative teacher should be able to help children see how inconvenient it is not to know the books of the Bible, Scripture verses to use in sharing Christ, or particular verses that will bring comfort or guidance. Yes, if children can see the value of learning verses, they will try to learn them. In one survey among 60 juniors, all of them said it was important to learn Scripture, but only a few of them were actually memorizing. The majority mentioned "not enough time," "hard for me to memorize," "no one to help me," "don't know which verses," and a variety of other answers.

If children are to memorize Scripture, we must carefully choose what will be useful to them. For example, how often does anyone need to know the names of the kings of Israel? Is the Easter story particularly important to memorize when a child can readily turn to a written account?

How shall we select Scripture for memorization? Sunday School curriculum can give you helpful verse selections. The old teaching attitude used to be, "Learn this and you'll like it." Try changing this order to "If you like it, memorize it." This change in direction means that Scripture must be sufficiently explained so that children will like it and want to learn it. Surely Psalms 23, 8, and 100, and many other portions easily fall into this category.

Elementary children enjoy choosing a topic and finding in a concordance verses related to it. Type the verses the children choose and let them memorize as many as they wish.

However, merely assigning memory work is not enough. If your children have several versions of the Bible and you want the entire group to enjoy repeating the passage together, use the selection from the version of your choice.

When you assign individual verses or longer selections, be sure that your assignments are "bite size," suited to the age of the children. Primaries can usually learn one or two verses at a time. Primary-juniors can handle three or four. Juniors may be able to learn three to five verses easily. A great deal has been written about the junior years being the "golden age of memory." They may be, but most juniors still need plenty of help to memorize.

It is possible to blunt a pupil's appreciation for a Bible passage by the very way it is taught—by dull, monotonous drilling, lack of enthusiasm, and absence of activity. On the other hand, it is possible to deepen appreciation for a passage if the teachers are willing to learn it, too. Always give the background for the Scripture passage. Read it for the children or let them hear a tape recording of it. Ask them what ideas they got from it, what the verses are saying to them, or what part of it they like best. Then assign the passage, suggesting how many verses can be learned at one time—not the entire selection.

Children should understand why it is important to memorize. As long as every child has a Bible and can read, he or she may not see any reason for learning

Bible verses. Ask some of your children why they think it would be a good idea to learn the passage. Make learning the verses a creative activity: Try flash cards, word strips on a flannel board or in a pocket chart, pictures to illustrate ideas, and sometimes pupil-prepared skits to act out the big ideas.

Once the children have learned a passage, review it often enough that it stays in their minds. Sometimes this can be done in a game-type activity before Sunday School begins. For example, hand one child a rubber ball. Ask the child to repeat as much of the passage as he or she can and then pass the ball to another child.

To read the Bible is good, but to memorize it is better. If, however, your group cannot memorize—and some children find memorizing very difficult—do ask juniors to mark their Bibles. Then they will know where particular verses are. As they read their Bibles, the Holy Spirit may remind them of the verses and use them in His ministry.

REACT

1. Are you experiencing Bible truth in your own life?
2. Is your reading of the Word meaningful to you?
3. What blessing have you received in the last week as a result of reading or memorizing Scripture?

ACT

1. If the concept was new to you, consider the idea of blending Bible facts with Bible truth.
2. Scan the Bible facts you include in a lesson to see how they help children understand Bible truth.

CHAPTER SEVEN
EVALUATING YOUR TEACHING

►Preparation and evaluation are vital elements in successful teaching. A teacher who prepares well, and then reviews what has happened in the classroom, is a teacher who will keep on growing and improving in the vital ministry of teaching boys and girls.

Most of us would agree that there is no more important calling than that of teaching the Word of God. How then do we prepare?

As a teacher, you cannot be ready to meet your pupils without first meeting God, the One whose work you do and the One you represent. Focus your attention on the Lord, being willing to learn from Him, the master Teacher. Keep a close relationship to Him in your study by seeing your own needs, including your need for cleansing. Then see your pupils' needs and pray for them. Too often a Sunday School teacher who does not prepare ahead of time is tempted to pray, "Lord, help me get through this lesson. Make it meaningful to the kids." It is fine to ask God's blessing on your presentation, but it is even more important to pray for your preparation, your pupils, and your presentation.

You should know the subject matter so well that it is a part of you. Before you teach, you will want to ask the Lord to teach you so that you may teach others. What does the lesson mean to you? You can never give others what you do not possess. If a Bible passage has little meaning for you, it will have even less meaning for your pupils! But if the lesson contains Bible truth that makes a change in your life—even a small difference—it will also make a mark on the lives of your pupils.

There is no other way to have a worthwhile lesson except through preparation. Your preparation may not be a duplicate of what you will really do in the classroom, but it will give you a blueprint to follow. Then you will be able to change your teaching plans as needed.

The A, B, C, D Plan

*A*sk the Lord to make the lesson real to you. Ask Him to give you new understanding, especially of familiar Bible events.

*B*egin early in the week so that the lesson can simmer in your mind, and you will be looking at your experiences in relation to the lesson.

*C*oncentrate on Bible study. Your understanding of Bible truth is the most important part of your lesson preparation. Begin with the Bible and meditate on it. Then use a Bible commentary for your personal study.

*D*etail your plan. After studying the Bible content, look at your teacher's book. It is your second teaching tool. In it there will be a lesson plan. But you will want to study the teacher's book and then make your own plan.

Your teacher's book should be the blueprint to help you translate your learning into terms, and by methods, your pupils will understand. Follow your teacher's book as a general rule. However, no Sunday School curriculum writer can visualize all situations. The ideas in your book are prepared for thousands of teachers who are teaching children in many locations with very different backgrounds and experiences. The writer's suggestions are trustworthy, but you can enhance the material by tailoring it for your own group of children.

Your lesson preparation should frequently include an evaluation of the place in which you teach. Are you satisfied with it? Regardless of how well you prepare at home, you need to consider the physical surroundings in which the children will learn. Are there ways to improve your room? Take a look at it as a child sees it. Does he or she see dirty windows, unattractive curtains, chipped paint, smudged walls, burned-out light bulbs, crooked pictures, out-of-season bulletin boards, or broken furniture? Will the child really believe that God's Word is real and Sunday School is important when his or her classroom is so inferior to a public school room? Have you made your room as attractive as possible?

Written Lesson Plans

Some teachers study the Bible, study the teacher's book, and then tell the class what they've studied. This is not teaching. You must translate your study into terms for the pupils, omitting some things you learned that you know are beyond the understanding of your pupils. A written outline will help you.

This outline will help you know how to budget your time for the various activities or parts of your lesson. A teacher who does not think through the parts of the lesson, estimating how long he or she will spend on each part, has a tendency to linger too long and then rush through the remainder of the material.

If time runs out, it is better to summarize what you have achieved and bring the lesson to a meaningful conclusion. Should you mention the time factor to children, they become acutely aware of it and find concentrating most difficult. Of course, if children are interested and are making meaningful comments, do not cut them off, saying, "We've got to finish the lesson." Concentrate on what they have said and summarize their thinking. Then help them relate it to their lives.

If you keep your written lesson plans, you should be able to see your lessons as a chain, leading to the unit goal. You will still teach each lesson for a specific response, but you will see how individual lessons relate to the overall objective. For example, you may have as a unit aim, "Knowing my freedom in Christ." Lessons in the unit may stress freedom from the power of sin, freedom from conformity to the crowd, and freedom to be a responsible person. Or a series of primary lessons may be on pleasing the Lord by being honest, by being kind, and by obeying.

In a written lesson plan, you will be following the four steps to learning to experience Bible truth as discussed in Chapter 4. Writing out a lesson plan is not busywork. Your outline will be most helpful. Include title of lesson, Scripture, aim of lesson, and memory verse, noting how the memory verse can be woven into the lesson. Then detail the four parts of the lesson—HOOK, BOOK, LOOK, and TOOK. Or you may want to list them as life need, Bible learning, Bible application, and life response.

1. *HOOK.* How will you begin? Do not review a former lesson as an approach, unless there is a purpose. Sometimes juniors appreciate a time line approach to

hold Bible events together. Or there may be times when you feel you need to link lessons through a common theme. For example, if your lessons are about Abraham, Moses, and Elijah, you could say, "How did God care for the Bible people we've been studying?" If you tie the lessons together, always do so with big, basic ideas.

Your approach will often be at the feeling level—beginning with their life need. How do your pupils *feel* about cheating, jealousy, or forgiveness? The "hook" may deal with a current problem in the lives of the pupils, events in the community, or in the life of an individual everyone knows. An adequate Sunday School curriculum will suggest a variety of approaches in the lessons.

Sometimes it is helpful to get information from the pupils to help you throughout the unit. Let's assume that your unit topic is God's care. On the first Sunday you might ask the pupils to give verbally (primaries) or in writing (primary-juniors and juniors) ideas about God's care. Ask them if they have any ideas about, or questions on, God's care for people. Give them time to think, and accept their contributions without comment. You have some idea, then, how your pupils feel. Check to see that you answer their questions throughout the unit.

2. *BOOK*. Always use the Bible in class. If you teach juniors, select some verses for the pupils to read. Do not choose more than a few verses, or you will spend most of the class time in reading and not have enough time for discussion. If you teach younger children, have your Bible open and read a few verses. It is important to let the children see that Sunday School is very literally Bible school—the Bible is the text.

To help you budget your time, allow about five minutes for your life-need approach (HOOK) to the lesson. Then at least two-thirds of your remaining time should be left for Bible learning. This includes the relevancy of the Bible to life. Your time will also include the "LOOK" of the lesson.

3. *LOOK.* This part of the lesson includes the personal implications for the children—the Bible application. Sometimes this is evident from the Bible content, but very often you may need to spend more time discussing the implications of Bible truth to life.

Often it is in the "BOOK" or "LOOK" section of the lesson that you will use different teaching methods or activities. If your teaching method involves materials, always practice with them ahead of time. Run the video or listen to the audio tape. If you are going to record, be sure that the machine is in working order. Tell the story aloud. Look at the visuals from the pupils' viewpoint. For example, it is possible to hold a flat picture at such an angle that it reflects a glare from the light. Or you may discover that a visual is too small to be seen from a distance of five or six feet.

4. *TOOK.* What is the pupil to do in light of the Bible truth? How will you help the children know how to make a life response? The application to life is very important, but if you sound like you are preaching or moralizing, the children will tune out. The best applications will come from the pupils themselves. As you become more skillful in wording questions, you will be able to help juniors arrive at their own conclusions. For example, you could say to a group of juniors, "How does the fact that the Israelites wanted a king help us?" No response from the children. You can ask another question, saying, "Okay, no one has an idea. Let's see if

we can take a giant step together. Why did the Israelites want a king? How were they choosing between God's way and their own way?" Then after several children have commented, see if the group can decide "How do people make that same choice today?"

If children can see the application and express it, your teaching will probably be stronger than if you have to explain. Primaries may not be able to do this most of the time, but juniors can be very discerning.

In linking Bible truth to life, do not embarrass any child. You would not appreciate the pastor's saying, "Dan, in view of the sermon, how are you going to change?" Children do not like being singled out either. But you can always say, "We may want to keep our thoughts to ourselves, but can you think of some way to trust the Lord this week? When we bow for prayer, will you tell the Lord how you are going to trust Him?" Whenever you have a closing prayer, state what you are expecting to happen. "We're going to pray, asking the Lord to help us (obey, trust Him for the end-of-school tests, etc.)." If children are willing to share their responses to Bible truth, be a good listener.

How Can You Evaluate Your Teaching?

As soon as possible after the session, think it through carefully and objectively. Reflect on what happened from the pupils' point of view. How did they respond? In evaluation, your concern is largely with what happens to the pupils. You may be tempted to decide that it was a good lesson because the children were quiet. There is nothing wrong with children being quiet, if they are listening and thinking. Then decide what seemed to go well according to the parts of the lesson.

HOOK: Were the children interested? Did you sense that they were with you and ready to discover something? Were they responsive, eager to make comments? Did your approach really represent a felt life need?

BOOK: Did they grasp significant personalities or circumstances and action in the Bible learning?

LOOK: Did the children see the relationship between the Bible event (or story) and life today? How did each child participate in this Bible application? When children did not participate, can you decide why they did not?

TOOK: Did the children seem to know how they should make a life response to the Lord in the light of Bible truth? On Sunday morning you can evaluate only what they understood. Your prayer throughout the week should be that the Lord will help each child live the Bible truth.

Did you let the children take off in directions that were not related to the lesson, but were only a matter of entertainment? How can you stop a recital of a TV episode or sports event? Try something like, "Jim, we'll be glad to listen if you can show us how what you're saying will help us with our lesson."

Did the visuals help make the lesson clear?

What did the children learn from the activities?

What Bible knowledge do you need to review with the children?

In the light of this lesson, how will you plan for next week? What children need a visit or contact by telephone?

Perhaps the most difficult part of your evaluation will be the application—the TOOK. It is not difficult to know how your application related to the pupils, but it is difficult to know whether the pupils will allow the

Holy Spirit to make changes in their lives. However, that is the pupil's choice—you can never make it for any child. Your responsibility is prayer—daily and fervent.

REACT

1. Does a written plan seem unimportant? Why? Have you tried it? If communicating God's Word is really important, what effort is too great for you to undertake?

ACT

If you want to be a growing teacher, there are a number of things you will want to do. Here are ways to help you improve week by week.

1. Keep working on the art of asking meaningful questions that lead to group discussion.
2. Work for variety in the methods you choose.
3. Try to allow more opportunities for the children to discover their own answers.
4. Visit a public school to watch teachers teach and children learn.
5. Ask someone to observe your teaching.
6. Plan to read at least two books in the next year that relate to your teaching.
7. Be willing to change your teaching plans to meet the pupils' needs.
8. Work at understanding every child.

CHAPTER EIGHT
RELATING TO CHILDREN

►We've already looked at many factors that are important in relating to boys and girls. But this factor is so vital in teaching that it's worth looking at carefully, and again.

It's not unusual at Sunday School conventions or in books on teaching to hear experts stress the importance of getting to know your pupils individually. If you've read carefully, you remember that I've stressed the same thing in this book. It's also helpful to establish a friendly relationship with your boys and girls beyond the classroom. Christian educators continue to encourage home visits, having one or two children over to your house, and doing fun things together as a class group beyond the Sunday School hour.

While I don't discourage this kind of involvement at all, I do want to suggest that your success as a teacher will hinge on the kind of relationship you develop with the children *in the classroom.*

Both Matthew and Sarah, a brother and sister in our church, have had Mrs. Ross as a teacher. She's an older lady, grandmotherly in fact. She has never visited Matthew or Sarah at home. She has never had them over to her house. Yet both Matt and Sarah dearly love Mrs. Ross. They have looked forward to Sundays, when they would have her for a teacher. Both children have been especially delighted with a small Christmas gift, or card when absent, just because it was from Mrs. Ross. Somehow, just in the short hour that the children spent with her each Sunday morning, a bond of love was established. It was a bond of love that motivated each child to want to attend—and to want to put into practice what Mrs. Ross teaches.

So the relationship that is established *during the class hour* is critical to the success of a teacher of boys and girls.

I once asked a group of Sunday School teachers to conduct an experiment. I asked each teacher to think of a person who'd had a positive personal or spiritual impact on his or her life. When those persons had been identified, I had the teachers share in groups of three, telling the others about each influential individual "so they can get to know him or her, too."

Then I drew five lines on the chalkboard. I listed qualities at the ends of these lines as follows:

Warm ______________________________ *Cold*

Close ______________________________ *Distant*

Knows Me ____________________ *Doesn't Know Me*

I Know Him (Her) __________ *Don't Know Him (Her)*

Two-Way Relationship ________________ *One-Way*

Next I asked each teacher to put a mental X on each line to describe his or her relationship with the influential person. As we discussed the results, we found that in nearly every case the relationships were marked by these qualities:

- ▶warmth rather than coldness
- ▶closeness rather than distance
- ▶feelings of really knowing and being known
- ▶two-way rather than one-way communication.

That last factor is especially important. It means that the persons who successfully influenced this group had *listened* rather than just talked.

Remember from an earlier chapter the description of the authoritarian teacher—one who insists kids remain quiet while he or she talks? The problem with this teaching style is that such a teacher may impart information, but is unlikely to influence his or her students!

Then there was the permissive teacher, who just talked with the kids about anything they wanted to bring up. This teacher may have an influence, but that influence is directionless. Our goal in teaching is to influence children to experience a personal relationship with Jesus by putting God's Word into practice.

The other teaching style discussed was the democratic. The democratic teacher made room in the class for the children to participate, while giving the participation structure and a teaching goal. Later chapters looked at how to structure Bible learning toward a goal.

Since you now understand these important ideas, let's go back and focus on how to develop the kind of relationship with boys and girls that encourages a directed yet democratic class process, the kind of relationship that Mrs. Ross has with her class. This kind of relationship lets you actually influence the lives of the children you teach as well as communicate important Bible truths.

Who Are You?

This is the first and most important issue. How do you see yourself when you relate to children?

There are a number of self-concepts that teachers have. One is the adult with children. There's nothing wrong with this image of yourself unless you think of adults as people with power and knowledge, and children as persons whose role in life is to submit and learn. Teachers with this view tend to be authoritarian in their teaching. They also tend to think of "covering the lesson" as their real task.

A closely related notion is that the teacher is a repository of information, and children are receptors. Teachers with this notion tend to think that their job is to make sure that children learn Biblical facts, and can give those facts back when asked. Again the class process tends to be authoritarian, as the teacher gives information and asks that the information be repeated by the boys and girls. This kind of teacher, like the first, is unlikely to develop any in-class relationship with boys and girls. Too much time is spent trying to maintain control; too many questions are impersonal rather than personal. And again the teacher thinks of his or her ministry in terms of how much can be covered, how many right answers can be learned.

What I want to suggest is that when you go into your classroom you think of yourself as an *adult friend.* In this role you can feel comfortable about guiding the class process. After all, adults are supposed to guide children. But you can also feel free to spend time on those little personal things that are appropriate in friendship. You can listen to the children share things that are important to them. You can share things that are happening to you. You can be happy for the good things in their lives, and can express real sympathy and concern for them in their problems. As the friendship relationship develops, boys and girls will be increasingly willing to talk about their experiences and feelings, and to explore how Bible truths can be applied.

But Is It Biblical?

One of the questions that teachers rightly ask is, "Is this a Scriptural role for a teacher?" Many of us have the impression that teachers are supposed to be authorities who teach an authoritative Word. We think that teachers are supposed to tell, and that learners are supposed to listen.

But when we look into the New Testament we make some fascinating discoveries. Actually, those who have been the most effective communicators of God's authoritative Word have also developed warm and close relationships with those they taught. While we could turn to others, let's just look for a moment at the apostle Paul. Here are a few passages in which he describes his relationship with believers in churches that he founded.

> *We have spoken freely to you, Corinthians, and opened wide our hearts to you. We are not withholding our affection from you . . . As a fair exchange—I speak as to my children—open wide your hearts also (II Cor. 6:11-13).*

> *As apostles of Christ we could have been a burden to you, but we were gentle among you, like a mother caring for her little children. We loved you so much that we were delighted to share with you not only the gospel of God but our lives as well, because you had become so dear to us. For you know that we dealt with each of you as a*

father deals with his own children, encouraging, comforting and urging you to live lives worthy of God, who calls you into his kingdom and glory (I Thess. 2:7, 8, 11, 12).

I thank God, whom I serve, as my forefathers did, with a clear conscience, as night and day I constantly remember you in my prayers. Recalling your tears, I long to see you, so that I may be filled with joy (II Tim. 1:3, 4).

It is clear from these passages that even the apostle Paul did not try to communicate God's truth in a relational vacuum. Even Paul, although he was an apostle with an apostle's authority, took time to become a true friend to those he taught.

Being a Friend

Sometimes adults who want to be friends with the children they teach don't quite know how. We may know how to relate to our adult friends. But what does being a friend to children mean?

In another book, *A Theology of Children's Ministry* (Zondervan, 1983), I've described children's descriptions of friendship behaviors. Here's a summary of their ideas:

1. *Taking turns.* "The one who has a bike will take turns. You let them take turns on a swing. They won't always be the boss; sometimes they'll let you decide. They'll take turns deciding."

2. *Conceding.* "Like if I wanted to play baseball and they wanted to play tennis . . . go along with them. You're playing and one of them cheats. The other one says, 'Okay,' he lets it go. He's always interested in what you are interested in and vice versa."

3. *Supporting the other.* "Take up for him if someone's picking on him. I sort of got in trouble and sort of blamed my friend. He would let it stay. If you did something wrong, they'll share the responsibility. If you get in trouble, he won't say you did it but stays with you. Won't leave you if you get in trouble."

4. *Explaining.* "If the person is stuck, show them the answer but tell them why it's the answer. If someone's being mean to that person, you can tell them not to and ask why. Talk over assignments. She gets in trouble with her parents; Jill gives her advice."

5. *Discussion.* "You know each other good and talk things out; talk problems out with you. You can talk to him and he'll talk to you. A friend wants to come and talk about your problem. A person you can talk to who will listen and tell you their problems."

6. *Reflecting values.* "When you have a problem, you can tell that friend and talk it over with him and he'll understand. She'll help you understand how you feel and give advice. Someone you can talk to . . . They can tell you what's wrong and what's right in a way. Then you can go to your friend and he would know what to say."

Perhaps these ideas can be summed up in just three words: Respect, listen, share.

One important factor here is to select a Sunday School curriculum in which the teaching process supports friendship development. Most curriculum writers today are aware of the characteristics and needs of children, and design their materials to match children's ways of thinking. But some materials clearly cast the teacher in an authoritarian role. How can you tell? A simple way is to look over a quarter of the materials you use (or are evaluating) and note the following important elements *toward the end* of the lesson plan. It is here, at the end, where application takes place, that talking and sharing are most important. It is here that the friendship relationship is most likely to be expressed. A curriculum in which the writers are sensitive to and try to encourage friendship relationships will do the following:

1. Have activities that carry out the stated aim.
2. Give priority to such activities. They are important to the whole lesson, not just an add-on "in case we have time."
3. Encourage exploring responses and life situations, allowing children to personalize their response.
4. Involve the children, helping them generate their own examples of situations in which the truths studied might apply.
5. Encourage the children to talk together about their own experiences and feelings.
6. Encourage open exploration of the meaning of what has been studied rather than force them toward "right answer" patterns of thought.

The Teacher As a Model

There is one additional aspect of the friendship relationship which is so important to develop as you teach boys and girls. It is this: In friendship teaching, the teacher becomes a living model or example to his or her class. Because the children come to know the teacher as a person and as a friend, they develop a desire to become like their teacher.

Jesus presented this as one of the results of successful teaching. "A student," Christ told His disciples, "is not above his teacher, but everyone who is fully trained will be like his teacher" (Luke 6:40).

What a challenge this is! God has called us to communicate ourselves *and* His truth.

While this concerns some teachers who feel inadequate or feel they are imperfect examples, it should encourage them instead. None of us is perfect yet. None of us is all he or she can be, or should be. Yet God's concern is that we are growing. God wants us to love Him, and to be able to say as the apostle Paul did, "I do not consider myself to have taken hold of it . . . I press on toward the goal to win the prize for which God has called me heavenward in Christ Jesus" (Phil. 3:13, 14). As long as we are growing in our relationships with God and with our boys and girls, God can use us in children's lives. In that sense, we can be good examples of what a Christian is supposed to be.

REACT

1. How many children in your class do you suppose think of you as a friend?

2. If your boys and girls were to describe their relationship with you on the continuum lines at the beginning of this chapter, where do you think they would put their mental check marks?

ACT

1. Another book in this Successful Teaching Series, *Teachers: Teaching with Love,* introduces you to a truly successful teacher. Why not read it, and note the ways in which Naomi built a friendship with her primary boys and girls?

2. Using the six criteria listed in this chapter, evaluate the curriculum you currently use—or another curriculum—for sensitivity to processes that develop an in-class friendship between teacher and children.

CHAPTER NINE
TEACHING FOR LIFE RESPONSE

▶If children can do it, let them! What are you doing for children that they can do for themselves? Make it a rule: Never do for a child any purposeful act that he or she can do for himself or herself.

The purpose of this chapter is to remind you that very little learning takes place unless the pupils participate. All learning involves activity on the part of the learner. Sometimes this activity is writing, drawing, telling, roleplay, or merely listening in order to think through questions and solve problems. But there must be some activity—some definite response—on the part of the child, or there will not be communication to bring about a changed life. Many teachers resent giving children equal-time rights in class. These are the people who equate talking with teaching.

If you really want to help children live Bible truth, you must communicate the Bible. And communication means both your giving and the pupils' receiving. Unless you allow time for pupils to respond and to become actively involved—to demonstrate their reaction—you may be scattering words into the atmosphere, hoping they will come to life in the pupils' minds. Good teaching means an involved teacher and an involved pupil.

Let's consider simple physical involvement first. Do you find yourself distributing pencils, hymnbooks, paper, or scissors? Why not let a child do it? Do you find yourself holding up a map or locating places on it? Could a child do it as well? Are you the only one who writes on the chalkboard? Can the children move flannel board figures for familiar stories? Could a child operate the videotape recorder? If you will let the children do all they can, their attitudes will improve and you will be teaching more effectively.

But physical involvement is not enough, and it is not always possible. However, every lesson can include mental involvement for all children. Let's see how this takes place in two junior classes.

The first teacher carefully prepares a mimeographed sheet of Bible verses describing God's love. He mounts the sheets on construction paper. Then he pastes seals of the head of Christ at the top of each sheet. On Sunday morning he distributes the sheets to his pupils. The group looks up every verse, even though this takes time. After someone reads a verse, the teacher comments on it. At the end of class the pupils carefully return the sheets to the teacher. They do not feel the sheets represent their work. Could this teacher have planned for more response, more involvement?

Another teacher in the same department prepares her lesson by using a concordance to find verses on God's love. She reads each verse to be sure the children are likely to understand it. She studies the verses that are particularly highlighted in her teacher's guide. Then she collects pencils with good points, along with her list of verses. At Sunday School she writes the Bible references on the chalkboard. She asks the children to volunteer to look up verses, writing initials next to the Bible references. Two children distribute the pencils. After a child reads a verse, the teacher asks another child to explain what the verse means to him or her. All are encouraged to make comments. After listening to the Bible verse and its explanation, the children write the Bible reference in their student books. Then they are encouraged to underline the verse in their Bibles. At the end of the class period, every child has a written record of verses on the topic; they have underlined some verses in their Bibles; and they have shared their thoughts on one or more verses.

Giving pupils an opportunity to become involved is not difficult, but it does take planning. As you think through your lessons, decide what the pupils can do. Perhaps you feel that you can do some things quicker and more efficiently. You probably can, but who learns by your doing? If your pupils leave the class with one big idea that means something to them—that can be lived out—you have communicated!

Why Ask Questions?

One of the most important things a teacher does is to ask questions. Why is this important? The pupils' responses to your questions show you the mental level on which they are operating. Questions allow each student to participate, and the answers the pupils give let you know whether it is time to move on to another point. If pupils have not understood, you must clarify or repeat information, rewording questions. If you do not use questions, you can teach an entire lesson, bringing it to what you think is a forceful conclusion, but you may fail because your children do not understand parts of the lesson.

What does it mean to assess the mental level of your

pupils? Do the questions demand your pupils *think* or merely feed back acceptable answers? Giving back rote answers, the very words you used, requires operating at only a low mental level. If you constantly accept factual answers, your students do not have to think about the meaning of the facts, putting them into a Biblical framework. Teachers who ask only factual questions may be keeping their pupils from finding the real meaning in the Scripture.

Let's take the example of baby Moses and his basket bed. (This may be oversimplification, but it may also be helpful.) You ask, "What kind of bed did baby Moses have?" "Who watched him?" "Who found him?" Primary children can give you one-word answers to all three questions. But suppose you ask, "How do you think Miriam felt when she was left alone with the baby?" "How do you think she felt (or what did she think) when the princess found the baby?" "How did she know what to do?"

As a general rule, "how" questions will mean more mental activity on the part of the pupils than "who" questions. You want your children—even first graders—to think for themselves, taking Bible truth into their own lives.

Questions help a teacher know whether the children have understood what has been said. A junior teacher was explaining "Moreover it is required in stewards, that a man be found faithful" (I Cor. 4:2, KJV). He listed some of the times when a person should be found faithful. Then he asked the boys to give their ideas. One boy said, "When the pilot wants him." Another answered, "He's supposed to think of the passengers before himself." Where did the boys get their ideas? Yes, the teacher had not thought it necessary to explain *steward*. In this true situation, the boys had decided these stewards were "male stewardesses," or flight attendants! Many, many illustrations could be given of primary children misunderstanding words, but older children misunderstand, too.

Questions help a teacher know what pupils understand. In the case of the teacher just mentioned, there was little point in making application to the boys' lives until they understood that *they* were stewards. Then they could think about faithfulness in terms of their fifth-grade existence. Use questions to help you know what you've accomplished and where you should go next. The pupils' responses to questions are a good check up for you.

How should a pupil respond to your questions? The average primary child has learned that Sunday School has to do with God, the Bible, Jesus, and "Be good." They know that you, the teacher, ask many questions that can be answered yes or no. They have also learned that they can read your nonverbal communication. If you look pleased when they start an answer, the chances are they're right—they are pleasing you. If you look impatient or concerned, they may decide not to continue with the answer or may say they don't know.

If you teach primary children, check your questions to see how many of them can be answered by "God," "the Bible," "Jesus," or "Be good." Yes-and-no questions give every child a 50 percent chance of being right in his or her response. Do your questions make a child think? With a little thought, you can make questions work for you in getting pupil response.

What do shotgun questions mean to the pupils? If you ask a question and then call on one pupil after another, what happens? "Who left Ur?" "Mary?" "John?" "Joe?" The shotgun approach leads the child to make one of these responses:

1. *I've got to think fast. It makes me nervous that she doesn't give me more time.*

2. *If I don't know, it doesn't matter because she'll ask someone else.*

3. *I hate it when he asks questions. It's like he's trying to trick someone.*

If your question is worth asking, it's worth giving the pupil time to think about it. Do not rush the children when you are asking thought questions. Some children discover that most teachers call on those who are most verbal. A sixth-grade girl did not answer any questions. One day I asked her why she never volunteered. I realized she knew the answers. She said, "Let the kids who want to. I don't care." Too often we call only on the children with wildly waving hands. How about the shy child? Do you sometimes say, "Well, Kevin, maybe you can't think of an answer right now, but we'll come back to you"? Do your questions give every child an opportunity to respond?

Have you tried letting pupils know that questions are meant to help them—not trip them up? Children respond much better to questions when they know the purpose is to help them. Give them an opportunity to ask questions, especially in review lessons.

Do your questions make the Bible more relevant to the pupils? Your questions can still be factual but meaningful. For example, "Where did David hide from King Saul?" requires a factual answer. But, "How did God take care of David when he was running from King Saul?" is probably more meaningful. To answer the second question the child has to imagine how David felt, possible places where he could hide, and God's care of him in several specific instances. The first question can be answered with cold, hard facts. The second question means some feeling on the part of the pupil. With a little practice you can ask questions that bring forth feelings instead of mere facts.

One more question about questions: Do you value a student's honest answer? How do you respond when a primary says he or she doesn't like Sunday School? What do you say if a junior is critical of the Bible (and some of them are)? Do your responses encourage a child to talk with you? One teacher found it necessary to talk privately with a junior boy about his behavior. The boy claimed Sunday School was boring, saying, "I get tired of hearing 'Let Jesus come into your heart.'" The teacher, who knew that he had not used that particular phrase, handled it this way.

Teacher: "Rob, I don't think you hear that very often, but let's assume you have heard it. Why would anyone say it?"

Rob: "Well, I guess if some kid doesn't know Jesus."

Teacher: "But how would you know that?"

Rob: "I guess you'd have to ask."

Teacher: "Rob, if you were the teacher, what would you ask?"

Rob: "Well, you'd have to say something about asking Jesus to be your Savior."

Teacher: "There are some boys in this class who have not asked Jesus to be their Savior. What do you think I should do to help them?"

As a result of this conversation, Rob suggested that he would pray for the boys. The teacher did not make Rob feel guilty. He tried to see the problem from Rob's point of view. If he had said, "Rob, you ought to be ashamed of yourself," what might have happened? Rob would have become defensive, he would have been more rebellious, and he would have decided that he was right—Sunday School *is* boring.

The response many teachers want most is a response

to a salvation invitation. Every teacher wants to know that each pupil in his or her charge has received Christ as Savior.

When Is a Child Ready to Receive the Savior?
While we cannot give a one-sentence answer to this question, we know that a teacher must be ready to relate God's offer of salvation to any child whenever the Holy Spirit directs. There is real danger in deciding children are not old enough or that they cannot understand. It is also dangerous to assume that all children in your group are Christians or are ready to become Christians. The teacher's responsibility is to make clear that Jesus came to be the Savior from sin for all who believe and put their trust in Him.

When a teacher tries to help children form right habits of conduct or Christian attitudes without giving them the desire to live out their love for the Savior, he or she is on dangerous ground. Salvation can never be put on as a cloak of righteousness until the heart is changed. We can never concentrate on the outward act instead of the inner drives—the motivation to want to live for the Lord.

This does not mean that a teacher constantly invites children to receive Christ without talking about living for Him. It does mean the teacher who knows his or her pupils will always keep in mind that some may not have received the Savior. He or she will never be guilty of making statements that give an unsaved child false security. Instead he or she will say that "many of us" or "most of us" love the Lord. He or she will not say, "You are a Christian, so you—" but, "If you are a Christian, you will want to give to the Lord."

Only the Holy Spirit knows the time when a child is ready to receive Christ. A teacher can and must sow the seed, but only the Holy Spirit will bring the results. Be ready to explain what receiving Jesus means, but always depend on the Holy Spirit to do the work.

Some children grow up in Christian homes and never know a time when they didn't love Jesus. It is wise to give these children an opportunity to openly affirm their love for Jesus and to celebrate the experience.

As a rule, a decision for Christ can be made any time a child is in the Primary, Primary-Junior, or Junior Department, or years later. However, it has been estimated that more than 50 percent of all Christians receive Christ by the time they are 12 years old.

Regarding leading a child to accept Christ, let's think about the negatives first; then we'll talk about the steps a teacher *should* take in helping a child understand salvation.

1. *Do not use fear as a motive.* It is true that unbelievers will not be with the Lord (Rev. 20:15), but a child who receives Christ because of the fear a teacher instills may not have saving faith. He or she may go through the prescribed actions, even repeating words, without really knowing Christ as Savior.

If a child asks what happens to people who do not believe, be truthful, saying that people who do not love the Lord will not be with Him—the Bible says they will be separated from God. A teacher who says, "If you don't ask Jesus to be your Savior, you will go to hell," is sure to get a response—but not necessarily one that is vital and lasting. When a child is old enough to get over his or her fear—and many do—he or she will probably become very hard about the whole matter.

2. *Do not give group invitations for everyone to stand or come forward.* When a leader gives a group invitation, it is too easy for every child to respond. Children come forward because they want the teacher's

approval or because everyone is doing it. If the Holy Spirit is dealing with a child, the child will do what is hard for him or her. He or she will stay after class or come to you individually.

3. *When a child has received Christ, do not reward him or her.* Pastors and teachers sometimes give the child a New Testament or a book. When this is done in front of other children, there is a tendency for others to respond to get the gift. Instead, take the New Testament or book to the child at his or her home.

Remember, these three basic, important ideas: (1) Do not shame or scare children into receiving salvation; (2) Do not make receiving the Savior too easy; and (3) Do not reward a child who responds to the invitation.

What *should* a teacher do to help a child receive Christ?

1. *Invite children to do something they would not normally want to do.* You may say, "If you want to know how Jesus can be your Savior, stay after class."
2. *Be sure that children have come of their own accord.* You may want to ask, "Why did you stay after class, Bobby? What did you want to talk about?" This line of friendly questioning helps you see what understanding the child has.
3. *Take plenty of time with the child.* Do not worry if he or she misses out on some other department activity.
4. *Be sure to use the Bible, but limit the verses you use.* Give children one verse they can understand and remember as assurance for what they have done.

What exactly should a teacher say? Explaining the following steps has helped many teachers lead a child to Christ:

1. God loves people very, very much.

2. All people have done wrong (Rom. 3:23). (Provide opportunity here for a child to feel sorry for his or her own sin and confess it to the Lord, asking forgiveness.)
3. God loves people so much that He sent His Son to die for every person, taking the punishment for that person's sin (Jn. 3:16 or I Cor. 15:3, 4).
4. If a person believes that Jesus died to take the punishment for his or her sin, and asks Jesus to be his or her Savior, that person can belong to God's family (Jn. 1:12). As a child of God, he or she will belong to God's family forever.
5. Have the child tell someone else.
6. If the child's parents would welcome word of his or her decision, be sure to talk to them. However, if a child is likely to face antagonism at home, you may want to let him or her talk with the parents, being sure that you are supporting him or her in prayer.
7. Be sure children know that whenever they do wrong they should go to the Lord, asking forgiveness (I Jn. 1:9). Bring this up sometime after the child's decision.

After children receive Christ, do not constantly remind them that they are Christians, using this fact as a disciplinary measure. "John, Christians don't cheat," or, "Christians don't tease." It is a sin against the children to use their testimony in this way.

A Word About Salvation Lessons

There are many object lessons and messages that appeal to young people and adults, but are not helpful to children. Remember, children in grades one through six are very literal people. They usually cannot understand symbolism! Perhaps they can give right answers, but research and experience indicate that they cannot really understand and apply symbolism in their own lives. Let's give a few examples of symbolism that these children *cannot* appreciate.

"The story is told of a foolish frog who refused to dive to the bottom of the pond and hibernate for the winter. So he sat on the bank. But one morning the pond's surface was frozen, and he could not dive. Boys and girls, you don't want to be like that frog, do you? One day it will be too late for you to ask Jesus to be your Savior."

What does the average primary get from this story? The usual response is one of sympathy for the frog!

Children understand body structure and would have many questions about the "heart" in this invitation: "Do you want Jesus to come into your heart and take out all the sin? He will fill that big empty space."

Word pictures of the Lord Jesus are Scriptural, but should be used only with young people or adults. Primaries cannot understand how Jesus can be Light, Bread, the Vine, the Door, or the Bridge to God. When older juniors begin to understand figurative language, these illustrations have meaning for them.

How Does a Child Grow Spiritually?

After a child becomes a Christian, you will see some behavioral changes, but do not expect perfection from him or her any more than you expect it from an adult. You will want the child to grow in reliance on the Lord, in frequent use of prayer, and in understanding and dependence on the Bible. As children grow in these ways, their behavior will change. Most children will grow slowly—they will not take giant steps in their Christian lives.

The child grows as a total person. If a child is a Christian, he or she does not receive a different body, though he or she is a new creature in Christ. The child is no longer under the power of sin, but is still a child. Sometimes adults associate sin with what is very normal behavior for a child. It is not helpful to children to meet their every negative action with, "If you want to please Jesus, you will . . ."

What can you do to help children grow spiritually? How can you expect them to grow? The following lists are indicative only. Your own observation should help you add to them.

What spiritually growing children may be like at age six:

- Like to hear Bible stories
- Feel a natural love for the Lord Jesus
- Say God made everything
- Recognize they have hard times and need to pray about them*

At age seven:

- Developing an ethical sense about self, though not always consistent
- Have ideas about acceptable behavior*
- Are able to make distinctions between what they are told and what they experience
- Have reasoning power that can be used in learning spiritual truth

At age eight:

- Can do limited Bible reading
- Are happiest with yes or no answers to moral problems*
- Have some concern for others and what happens to them*
- Want very definite information about God*

At age nine:

- ▶ Can be challenged to cooperate
- ▶ Can be more objective about themselves
- ▶ Teacher is important*
- ▶ Is ready to accept some historical information about Bible
- ▶ Need help in developing into the kind of persons they want to become*

At age ten:

- ▶ Can learn many facts but need help in seeing how Bible truth applies*
- ▶ Should be encouraged to read Bible for themselves*
- ▶ Prayer can become very meaningful
- ▶ May want to share their faith

At age eleven:

- ▶ Have many new values they are trying and testing*
- ▶ Tend to judge right and wrong by their feelings*
- ▶ Can relate some Bible truth to themselves without help
- ▶ Need help from Christian teachers in dealing with their emotional reactions to various situations*

Did you notice one or more asterisks (*) in each list? If you are growing as a teacher in your listening power, you should be able to give needed help in these particular areas. Always use guided conversation and questions to help children find their own answers. By all means, walk with the children—not ahead of them.

Suppose a sixth-grade boy is working on evaluating right and wrong by his feelings, using the example of whether to keep money found on the floor of the school lunchroom. He says, "But the person who lost it would never have found the money anyway." What do you say? Perhaps some would say, "God sees you." This is not news to a Sunday School child; he still feels it is okay to keep the money. Approach him at the feeling level by saying, "You thought it was all right to do because you felt comfortable about it? What made you feel that way?" Your questions and conversation must be guided by his answers, but you may be able to continue at the feeling level by saying, "If you had been the person who lost the money, how might you feel?"

There are times when you will have to end a conversation with a child without coming to the conclusion you would like. But the important thing to remember is that the child wants to know you understand. If you think an older child, as in the found-money example, really does not know what to do, you may want to ask, "Are you wondering what you should do?" Then express your opinion, but do not condemn the child if he or she does not act on it. Trust the Holy Spirit to work in the child's life. Your job is to pray, remembering that all believers grow through the power of the Holy Spirit as they give themselves over to Him. No teacher can force a child's spiritual growth.

REACT

How can your plans for pupil involvement provide children with motivation to study, to learn, and to want to experience Bible truth?

ACT

Record your next teaching session. As you listen to the tape or cassette, evaluate your questions, pupil comments, and your reactions. Did you ask good, involving questions? Did you find any indication of pupil interests or needs which you ignored?

CHAPTER TEN
AFTER SUNDAY MINISTRY

▶"Therefore, my dear brothers, stand firm. Let nothing move you. Always give yourselves fully to the work of the Lord, because you know that your labor in the Lord is not in vain" (I Cor. 15:58).

This familiar quotation from I Corinthians is more than an encouragement to teachers. What exhortation do you find in it? What we neglect to do for the Lord is wasted. Take a look at two teachers who have read this book, or one similar to it.

One teacher closes the book, shuts his eyes, and begins to think of his class. He can see the dingy, torn curtains in his classroom. They surely need to be replaced! He imagines the children's faces eager and happy as he suggests planning and working out a skit—something he has never done.

He wonders, "Would my children be able to make an 'I Will Trust' scrapbook? We've never tried anything like that, and it does sound like quite a job. The children could come here to the house for an evening of fun and work." But then he looks at the clock. It's late, and tomorrow is a busy day with work to do and many errands to run.

"Yes," he says aloud, "it would be fun to try out new methods, to really get to know the kids. But I don't have time. The story for Sunday is the Good Samaritan. The kids like it, and I can make it plenty exciting. Maybe someday I'll have time to really work at teaching."

The second teacher puts her book aside and smiles as she thinks of the interest her juniors would show in making their own time line. Study of the Old Testament kings hasn't always been interesting, but if she could help her pupils see that those men were real, they would better appreciate God's dealings with His people!

This teacher begins looking into some of the minor prophets. She knows her pupils would not learn from reading these books of the Bible for themselves, but she could find some key verses that would have meaning for juniors. She goes to her teaching resource kit. Enrichment activities in the kit give suggestions for a time line.

This teacher proceeds to work for two evenings to prepare for 15 minutes of class time! Worth it? Yes! Her juniors are fascinated with the time line. They see how God always had a messenger ready to speak His Word to the people. One boy says, "Wasn't God patient? Why didn't He punish those people?"

The teacher knows her juniors sense God's faithfulness and justice in His dealings with Old Testament people. The children gather around tables to complete their time lines. They have a lot to say and ask when they see a familiar name on the time line.

After the class session, this teacher evaluates her teaching. She thanks the Lord for what she has learned. Then she prays for the juniors, remembering their specific needs. She thinks about the needs she saw as the juniors talked. Surely an important need for them was patience! She can hardly wait to get started preparing for the next Bible lesson.

Your teaching is more than a Sunday job! True, you meet with a specific group of children once a week to communicate Bible truth, but teaching is more than that. You are probably one of the few people in your community interested in the spiritual welfare of a particular group of children—the children you teach. Have you ever thought of yourself as a coach? A coach cannot play the game for the players; you cannot live the Christian life for your students, but you are very much concerned with their living, their experiencing Bible truths. As a coach you are helping your pupils develop their skills and know-how to perform in the game of life. You should be one who is available, one to whom they can come with problems, and the one who has some suggestions for solving those problems.

A teacher who sees Sunday School as only a Sunday morning job should ask the Lord for a vision of what teaching can be. If nothing the teacher does for the Lord is ever wasted, can he or she ever do too much for the Lord?

Every teacher worthy of the calling is overwhelmed by the task! But the Lord does not expect you to face it in your own strength. He gives the wisdom, patience, understanding, and physical strength you need to grow as a person, to grow in teaching skill, and to grow in understanding children.

Teaching in the Sunday School is a demanding job, because we are not teaching people to write, read, or repair cars. We are teaching people how to live!

This book has told you a great deal about in-class teaching. But what about the contacts you make outside of class? What contacts should you make? Do the children like it when the teacher comes to call? How can you let a child know that he or she is important to you?

Are your children really important to you? In what way? Do you pray for each child every day? Do you think of the children as individuals when you prepare your lesson, selecting questions or comments to direct to each child?

Do you have your children in mind when you dress for Sunday School? You are the best audiovisual that will ever be in your classroom! Remember, boys and girls enjoy your colorful tie or your bright new dress. Keep in mind, however, that your clothing should represent about the same economic level as the children you teach. Do not overdress, because if the children feel you are on a much higher economic level, it can be a barrier between you.

In addition to Sunday morning, how often do you bring your children together for fun or for a service project? Most junior teachers should try to have the class together once a quarter—every three months. Primary and primary-junior teachers may want to limit class parties to two or three times a year. Parties are important to boys and girls and should be part of the church program for them.

If you gather together for fun, check out your ideas with the children ahead of time. Be sure you are planning games they will enjoy. If you gather for a service project, be sure that the children know the purpose of the project. Boys and girls may be challenged to serve the Lord in ways like these:

- Baking cookies for a shut-in or lonely person.
- Sorting outdated Sunday School papers to send to missionaries or a children's home.

- Doing work at the church building—dusting, raking, sorting handcraft materials, etc.
- Doing lawn work for an elderly or disabled person.
- Helping with a newspaper drive, selling the paper, and giving the money for a missionary project.
- Making and delivering tray favors or special day cards for nursing homes.
- Putting on a program at a convalescent home in your area—singing, reciting Scripture, and perhaps telling a flannel board story.
- Assisting with community-sponsored projects such as picking up litter.

Decide what your children can do. Then talk with the boys and girls, suggesting possibilities. If the children help decide on the project, it will be much more meaningful to them.

One junior superintendent presented a one-week challenge to collect money for a Christian relief agency. She asked the children to vote if they were willing to participate. Any child casting a yes vote would do his or her best to bring money the following Sunday. Every child in the department contributed!

To see how children think and react, look at the contributions of three children to that project. One nine-year-old girl gave $5 which she had saved for something she wanted. She told her mother, "I just couldn't enjoy it when I think of the children who are hungry." The wise mom let her child sacrifice. She did not buy what the child had wanted or give her money toward it. She let her daughter give joyfully.

Two sixth-grade boys, good friends, set out to see how much they could turn in. They raked leaves for three afternoons—a job they despised. They also tried to make collections among neighbors and friends. As a result, the two friends turned in $25.

What do you do about absentees? Are you making phone calls and sending notes to keep the child's interest? One teacher thought Jamie was away for the weekend. She assumed he was sick the second week. By the time she phoned, after three weeks, she was horrified to discover that Jamie had been ill, hospitalized, and was just beginning to feel better. When she talked with the boy's father, there was very little she could say to convince him of her interest in the child.

By contrast, in another home the teacher was the first one called when a grandparent was seriously ill. If pupils and their families feel you are really interested, they may turn to you as a spiritual counselor and friend.

What attitude do you take to the newcomer or visitor? The ministry of your Sunday School will be much more effective if every teacher can say, "John visited my class. He is my responsibility until I know that he is enrolled in another class, here or in another church."

When you read the local newspaper, do you look for news of your pupils? Has someone in your class made the honor roll, been in a school play, earned a place on the baseball team, or appeared in a recital? These events are important to the children. You should recognize their achievements with a phone call, note, or special mention before Sunday School.

Do children enjoy your visits in their homes? Yes and no. Why are you making the visit? If it is only to check up on the child, he or she may sense this and wish you had not come. If you are visiting the home because you are *sincerely* interested in the child and family, he or she will enjoy it. Primaries and young juniors are usually pleased to have a teacher call, and say so. Older juniors will be reluctant to show their appreciation, but they will feel your interest.

Making It Happen

How do you plan to improve as a teacher in the year ahead? What about your study of God's Word? Will you enroll in a correspondence course, church study group, or neighborhood Bible class? What books will you read to help you teach?

Better teaching does not just happen! Variety of methods, new projects, and various activities will make some changes, but they do not always mean better teaching. If you are sincerely concerned with helping pupils find Christ and then in living for Him, you will evaluate all your teaching in the light of these two tremendous goals.

REACT

1. Think over the material presented in this book. Has anything you have read caused you to change your motives for teaching?
2. What aspect of the book struck you as being the most beneficial to yourself personally and yourself as a teacher?

ACT

1. Based on this book, choose one thing you intend to begin or change with your next teaching session.
2. Share with another teacher or a friend some of the most important things you've learned from this book; ask him or her to help you carry out any new plans you have for your class.